W9-BME-203

SCOTT FORESMAN • ADDISON WESLEY

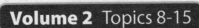
**Volume 2** Topics 8-15

## Authors

**Randall I. Charles**
Professor Emeritus
Department of Mathematics
San Jose State University
San Jose, California

**Jennifer Bay-Williams**
Professor of Mathematics Education
College of Education and Human
Development
University of Louisville
Louisville, Kentucky

**Robert Q. Berry, III**
Associate Professor of
Mathematics Education
Department of Curriculum,
Instruction and Special Education
University of Virginia
Charlottesville, Virginia

**Janet H. Caldwell**
Professor of Mathematics
Rowan University
Glassboro, New Jersey

**Zachary Champagne**
Assistant in Research
Florida Center for Research in Science,
Technology, Engineering, and
Mathematics (FCR-STEM)
Jacksonville, Florida

**Juanita Copley**
Professor Emerita, College of Education
University of Houston
Houston, Texas

**Warren Crown**
Professor Emeritus of Mathematics
Education
Graduate School of Education
Rutgers University
New Brunswick, New Jersey

**Francis (Skip) Fennell**
L. Stanley Bowlsbey Professor
of Education and Graduate and
Professional Studies
McDaniel College
Westminster, Maryland

**Karen Karp**
Professor of Mathematics Education
Department of Early Childhood and
Elementary Education
University of Louisville
Louisville, Kentucky

**Stuart J. Murphy**
Visual Learning Specialist
Boston, Massachusetts

**Jane F. Schielack**
Professor of Mathematics
Associate Dean for Assessment and
Pre K-12 Education, College of Science
Texas A&M University
College Station, Texas

**Jennifer M. Suh**
Associate Professor for
Mathematics Education
George Mason University
Fairfax, Virginia

**Jonathan A. Wray**
Mathematics Instructional Facilitator
Howard County Public Schools
Ellicott City, Maryland

PEARSON

Glenview, Illinois     Boston, Massachusetts     Chandler, Arizona     Hoboken, New Jersey

## Mathematicians

**Roger Howe**
Professor of Mathematics
Yale University
New Haven, Connecticut

**Gary Lippman**
Professor of Mathematics and
Computer Science
California State University, East Bay
Hayward, California

## ELL Consultants

**Janice R. Corona**
Independent Education Consultant
Dallas, Texas

**Jim Cummins**
Professor
The University of Toronto
Toronto, Canada

**Debbie Crisco**
Math Coach
Beebe Public Schools
Beebe, Arkansas

**Kathleen A. Cuff**
Teacher
Kings Park Central School District
Kings Park, New York

**Erika Doyle**
Math and Science Coordinator
Richland School District
Richland, Washington

## Common Core State Standards Reviewers

**Susan Jarvis**
Math and Science Curriculum Coordinator
Ocean Springs Schools
Ocean Springs, Mississippi

**Velvet M. Simington**
K–12 Mathematics Director
Winston-Salem/Forsyth County Schools
Winston-Salem, North Carolina

ISBN-13: 978-0-328-82742-8
ISBN-10: 0-328-82742-8

16  19

You'll be using these digital resources throughout the year!

# Digital Resources

## Go to PearsonRealize.com

### MP
**Math Practices Animations** to play anytime

### Glossary
**Animated Glossary** in English and Spanish

### Help
**Another Look Homework Video** for extra help

### ACTIVe-book
**Student Edition** online for showing your work

### Solve
**Solve & Share** problems plus math tools

### Tools
**Math Tools** to help you understand

### Games
**Math Games** to help you learn

### Learn
**Visual Learning Animation Plus** with animation, interaction, and math tools

### Assessment
**Quick Check** for each lesson

### eText
**Student Edition** online

**PEARSON**
**realize**™ Everything you need for math anytime, anywhere

# Contents

## KEY

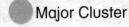

● Major Cluster

● Supporting Cluster

● Additional Cluster

The content is organized to focus on Common Core clusters.

For a list of clusters, see Volume 1 pages F13–F16.

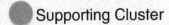
**Digital Resources at PearsonRealize.com**

And remember your eText is available at PearsonRealize.com!

## TOPICS

1  Solve Addition and Subtraction Problems to 10

2  Fluently Add and Subtract Within 10

3  Addition Facts to 20: Use Strategies

4  Subtraction Facts to 20: Use Strategies

5  Work with Addition and Subtraction Equations

6  Represent and Interpret Data

7  Extend the Counting Sequence

8  Understand Place Value

9  Compare Two-Digit Numbers

10  Use Models and Strategies to Add Tens and Ones

11  Use Models and Strategies to Subtract Tens

12  Measure Lengths

13  Time

14  Reason with Shapes and Their Attributes

15  Equal Shares of Circles and Rectangles

PearsonRealize.com

You can think about numbers in different ways. 23 is 2 groups of 10 and 3 left over.

# TOPIC 8
# Understand Place Value

Math and Science Project. . . . . . . . . . . . . . . . . . . . . . . . . . . . . . . . . . . . . 445
Review What You Know. . . . . . . . . . . . . . . . . . . . . . . . . . . . . . . . . . . . . . 446
Vocabulary Cards. . . . . . . . . . . . . . . . . . . . . . . . . . . . . . . . . . . . . . . . . . 447

**8-1**    **Make Numbers 11 to 19** . . . . . . . . . . . . . . . . . . . . . . . . . . 449
1.NBT.B.2b, 1.NBT.B.2a, MP.4, MP.5, MP.7, MP.8

**8-2**    **Numbers Made with Tens**. . . . . . . . . . . . . . . . . . . . . . . . 455
1.NBT.B.2a, 1.NBT.B.2c, MP.2, MP.3, MP.6, MP.8

**8-3**    **Count with Groups of Tens and Leftovers** . . . . . . . . . . . . 461
1.NBT.B.2, MP.1, MP.4, MP.5, MP.8

**8-4**    **Tens and Ones**. . . . . . . . . . . . . . . . . . . . . . . . . . . . . . . 467
1.NBT.B.2, MP.2, MP.4, MP.7, MP.8

**8-5**    **Continue with Tens and Ones** . . . . . . . . . . . . . . . . . . . . 473
1.NBT.B.2, MP.2, MP.4, MP.5, MP.8

**8-6**    **MATH PRACTICES AND PROBLEM SOLVING**
**Look For and Use Structure**
MP.7 Also MP.2, MP.3, 1.NBT.B.2. . . . . . . . . . . . . . . . . . . . . . . . . . 479

Fluency Practice Activity. . . . . . . . . . . . . . . . . . . . . . . . . . . . . . . . . . . . . 485
Vocabulary Review. . . . . . . . . . . . . . . . . . . . . . . . . . . . . . . . . . . . . . . . . 486
Reteaching. . . . . . . . . . . . . . . . . . . . . . . . . . . . . . . . . . . . . . . . . . . . . . 487
Topic Assessment . . . . . . . . . . . . . . . . . . . . . . . . . . . . . . . . . . . . . . . . . 489
Topic Performance Assessment. . . . . . . . . . . . . . . . . . . . . . . . . . . . . . . . 491

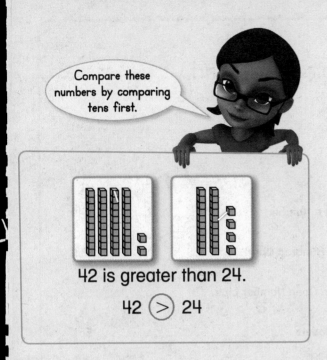

Compare these numbers by comparing tens first.

42 is greater than 24.

42 $>$ 24

# TOPIC 9
## Compare Two-Digit Numbers

Math and Science Project. . . . . . . . . . . . . . . . . . . . . . . . . . . . . . . . . . . 493
Review What You Know. . . . . . . . . . . . . . . . . . . . . . . . . . . . . . . . . . . . 494
Vocabulary Cards. . . . . . . . . . . . . . . . . . . . . . . . . . . . . . . . . . . . . . . . 495

**9-1** **I More, I Less; 10 More, 10 Less** . . . . . . . . . . . . . . . . . . . . . 497
I.NBT.B.3, I.NBT.C.5, MP.2, MP.5, MP.6, MP.8

**9-2** **Make Numbers on a Hundred Chart** . . . . . . . . . . . . . . . . . . . . . 503
I.NBT.C.5, MP.3, MP.5, MP.7

**9-3** **Compare Numbers**. . . . . . . . . . . . . . . . . . . . . . . . . . . . . . . . . . 509
I.NBT.B.3, MP.I, MP.2, MP.4, MP.6

**9-4** **Compare Numbers with Symbols (>, <, =)** . . . . . . . . . . . . . . . . . . 515
I.NBT.B.3, MP.2, MP.3, MP.6

**9-5** **Compare Numbers on a Number Line**. . . . . . . . . . . . . . . . . . . . 521
I.NBT.B.3, MP.I, MP.2, MP.4, MP.5

**9-6** **MATH PRACTICES AND PROBLEM SOLVING**
**Make Sense and Persevere**
MP.I Also MP.2, MP.3, I.NBT.B.3. . . . . . . . . . . . . . . . . . . . . . . . . . 527

Fluency Practice Activity. . . . . . . . . . . . . . . . . . . . . . . . . . . . . . . . . . 533
Vocabulary Review. . . . . . . . . . . . . . . . . . . . . . . . . . . . . . . . . . . . . . 534
Reteaching. . . . . . . . . . . . . . . . . . . . . . . . . . . . . . . . . . . . . . . . . . . . 535
Topic Assessment . . . . . . . . . . . . . . . . . . . . . . . . . . . . . . . . . . . . . . 537
Topic Performance Assessment. . . . . . . . . . . . . . . . . . . . . . . . . . . . 539

For every ten you add, move down 1 row in the hundred chart.

| 1 | 2 | 3 | 4 | 5 | 6 | 7 | 8 | 9 | 10 |
|---|---|---|---|---|---|---|---|---|---|
| 11 | 12 | 13 | 14 | 15 | 16 | 17 | 18 | 19 | 20 |
| 21 | 22 | 23 | 24 | 25 | 26 | 27 | 28 | 29 | 30 |

# TOPIC 10
## Use Models and Strategies to Add Tens and Ones

Math and Science Project. . . . . . . . . . . . . . . . . . . . . . . . . . . . . . . . . . . . . . . . 541
Review What You Know. . . . . . . . . . . . . . . . . . . . . . . . . . . . . . . . . . . . . . . . . 542

**10-1  Add Tens Using Models** . . . . . . . . . . . . . . . . . . . . . . . . . . . . . . . . 543
I.NBT.C.4, MP.1, MP.2, MP.4, MP.8

**10-2  Mental Math: Ten More Than a Number** . . . . . . . . . . . . . . . . . . . . 549
I.NBT.C.5, MP.2, MP.3, MP.4, MP.7

**10-3  Add Tens and Ones Using a Hundred Chart**. . . . . . . . . . . . . . . . . . 555
I.NBT.C.4, MP.4, MP.5, MP.7

**10-4  Add Tens and Ones Using an Open Number Line**. . . . . . . . . . . . . . 561
I.NBT.C.4, MP.2, MP.4, MP.6

**10-5  Add Tens and Ones Using Models** . . . . . . . . . . . . . . . . . . . . . . . . 567
I.NBT.C.4, MP.3, MP.4, MP.7

**10-6  Make a Ten to Add** . . . . . . . . . . . . . . . . . . . . . . . . . . . . . . . . . . . . 573
I.NBT.C.4, MP.2, MP.4, MP.5, MP.6

**10-7  Add Using Place Value**. . . . . . . . . . . . . . . . . . . . . . . . . . . . . . . . . . 579
I.NBT.C.4, MP.1, MP.2, MP.3, MP.4

**10-8  Practice Adding Using Strategies**. . . . . . . . . . . . . . . . . . . . . . . . . . 585
I.NBT.C.4, I.NBT.C.5, MP.2, MP.3, MP.4, MP.5

**10-9  MATH PRACTICES AND PROBLEM SOLVING
Model with Math**
MP.4 Also MP.2, MP.3, MP.5, I.NBT.C.4 . . . . . . . . . . . . . . . . . . . . . . . . . 591

Fluency Practice Activity. . . . . . . . . . . . . . . . . . . . . . . . . . . . . . . . . . . . . . . . 597
Vocabulary Review. . . . . . . . . . . . . . . . . . . . . . . . . . . . . . . . . . . . . . . . . . . . 598
Reteaching. . . . . . . . . . . . . . . . . . . . . . . . . . . . . . . . . . . . . . . . . . . . . . . . . . 599
Topic Assessment . . . . . . . . . . . . . . . . . . . . . . . . . . . . . . . . . . . . . . . . . . . . 603
Topic Performance Assessment. . . . . . . . . . . . . . . . . . . . . . . . . . . . . . . . . . 607

Contents

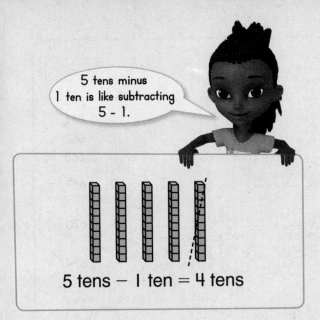

5 tens minus 1 ten is like subtracting 5 - 1.

5 tens − 1 ten = 4 tens

## TOPIC 11
## Use Models and Strategies to Subtract Tens

Math and Science Project. . . . . . . . . . . . . . . . . . . . . . . . . . . . . . . . . . . 609
Review What You Know. . . . . . . . . . . . . . . . . . . . . . . . . . . . . . . . . . . . . 610

**11-1** **Subtract Tens Using Models** . . . . . . . . . . . . . . . . . . . . . . . . . . . 611
1.NBT.C.5, 1.NBT.C.6, MP.1, MP.2, MP.6

**11-2** **Subtract Tens Using a Hundred Chart** . . . . . . . . . . . . . . . . . . . . 617
1.NBT.C.5, 1.NBT.C.6, MP.3, MP.5, MP.6, MP.8

**11-3** **Subtract Tens Using an Open Number Line** . . . . . . . . . . . . . . . . 623
1.NBT.C.5, 1.NBT.C.6, MP.4, MP.5, MP.8

**11-4** **Use Addition to Subtract Tens** . . . . . . . . . . . . . . . . . . . . . . . . . . . 629
1.NBT.C.6, MP.2, MP.3, MP.4, MP.7

**11-5** **Mental Math: Ten Less Than a Number** . . . . . . . . . . . . . . . . . . . . 635
1.NBT.C.5, MP.1, MP.2, MP.7

**11-6** **Use Strategies to Practice Subtraction**. . . . . . . . . . . . . . . . . . . . . 641
1.NBT.C.5, 1.NBT.C.6, MP.3, MP.4, MP.5

**11-7** **MATH PRACTICES AND PROBLEM SOLVING**
**Model with Math**
MP.4 Also MP.1, MP.5, 1.NBT.C.5, 1.NBT.C.6 . . . . . . . . . . . . . . . . . 647

Fluency Practice Activity. . . . . . . . . . . . . . . . . . . . . . . . . . . . . . . . . . . . 653
Vocabulary Review. . . . . . . . . . . . . . . . . . . . . . . . . . . . . . . . . . . . . . . . 654
Reteaching . . . . . . . . . . . . . . . . . . . . . . . . . . . . . . . . . . . . . . . . . . . . . . 655
Topic Assessment . . . . . . . . . . . . . . . . . . . . . . . . . . . . . . . . . . . . . . . . 657
Topic Performance Assessment. . . . . . . . . . . . . . . . . . . . . . . . . . . . . . 659

The crayon is 2 cubes long.

# TOPIC 12
## Measure Lengths

Math and Science Project. . . . . . . . . . . . . . . . . . . . . . . . . . . . . . . . . . . . . . . . 661
Review What You Know. . . . . . . . . . . . . . . . . . . . . . . . . . . . . . . . . . . . . . . . . . 662
Vocabulary Cards. . . . . . . . . . . . . . . . . . . . . . . . . . . . . . . . . . . . . . . . . . . . . . 663

**12-1** **Compare and Order by Length**. . . . . . . . . . . . . . . . . . . . . . . . . 667
I.MD.A.I, MP.2, MP.6, MP.8

**12-2** **Indirect Measurement** . . . . . . . . . . . . . . . . . . . . . . . . . . . . . . . . 673
I.MD.A.I, MP.I, MP.2, MP.5, MP.7

**12-3** **Use Units to Measure Length** . . . . . . . . . . . . . . . . . . . . . . . . . . 679
I.MD.A.2, MP.4, MP.5

**12-4** **Continue to Measure Length** . . . . . . . . . . . . . . . . . . . . . . . . . . 685
I.MD.A.I, I.MD.A.2, MP.3, MP.4, MP.6

**12-5** **MATH PRACTICES AND PROBLEM SOLVING**
**Use Appropriate Tools**
MP.5 Also MP.3, MP.8, I.MD.A.2 . . . . . . . . . . . . . . . . . . . . . . . . . . . . . 691

Fluency Practice Activity. . . . . . . . . . . . . . . . . . . . . . . . . . . . . . . . . . . . . . . . 697
Vocabulary Review. . . . . . . . . . . . . . . . . . . . . . . . . . . . . . . . . . . . . . . . . . . . 698
Reteaching. . . . . . . . . . . . . . . . . . . . . . . . . . . . . . . . . . . . . . . . . . . . . . . . . . 699
Topic Assessment . . . . . . . . . . . . . . . . . . . . . . . . . . . . . . . . . . . . . . . . . . . . 701
Topic Performance Assessment. . . . . . . . . . . . . . . . . . . . . . . . . . . . . . . . . . 703

The minute hand and the hour hand can help you tell time on a clock.

minute hand

hour hand

# TOPIC 13
## Time

Math and Science Project . . . . . . . . . . . . . . . . . . . . . . . . . . . . . . . . . . . . . . . 705
Review What You Know . . . . . . . . . . . . . . . . . . . . . . . . . . . . . . . . . . . . . . . . . 706
Vocabulary Cards . . . . . . . . . . . . . . . . . . . . . . . . . . . . . . . . . . . . . . . . . . . . . 707

**13-1**   **Understand the Hour and Minute Hands** . . . . . . . . . . . . . . . . 709
1.MD.B.3, MP.1, MP.5, MP.6, MP.7

**13-2**   **Tell and Write Time to the Hour** . . . . . . . . . . . . . . . . . . . . . . . 715
1.MD.B.3, MP.2, MP.6, MP.7, MP.8

**13-3**   **Tell and Write Time to the Half Hour** . . . . . . . . . . . . . . . . . . . 721
1.MD.B.3, MP.2, MP.3, MP.6, MP.7

**13-4**   **MATH PRACTICES AND PROBLEM SOLVING**
**Reasoning**
MP.2 Also MP.3, MP.4, MP.8, 1.MD.B.3 . . . . . . . . . . . . . . . . . . . . . 727

Fluency Practice Activity . . . . . . . . . . . . . . . . . . . . . . . . . . . . . . . . . . . . . . . . 733
Vocabulary Review . . . . . . . . . . . . . . . . . . . . . . . . . . . . . . . . . . . . . . . . . . . . 734
Reteaching . . . . . . . . . . . . . . . . . . . . . . . . . . . . . . . . . . . . . . . . . . . . . . . . . . 735
Topic Assessment . . . . . . . . . . . . . . . . . . . . . . . . . . . . . . . . . . . . . . . . . . . . 737
Topic Performance Assessment . . . . . . . . . . . . . . . . . . . . . . . . . . . . . . . . . . 739

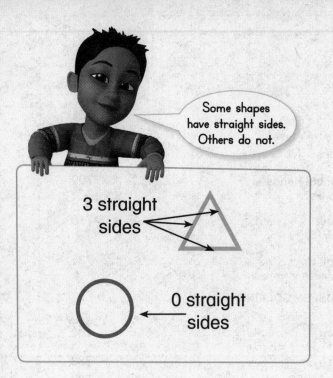

Some shapes have straight sides. Others do not.

3 straight sides

0 straight sides

# TOPIC 14
## Reason with Shapes and Their Attributes

Math and Science Project. . . . . . . . . . . . . . . . . . . . . . . . . . . . . . . . . . . . . . . . . 741
Review What You Know. . . . . . . . . . . . . . . . . . . . . . . . . . . . . . . . . . . . . . . . . . 742
Vocabulary Cards. . . . . . . . . . . . . . . . . . . . . . . . . . . . . . . . . . . . . . . . . . . . . . 743

**14-1**   **Use Attributes to Define Two-Dimensional (2-D) Shapes**. . . . . . . . . . 747
I.G.A.1, MP.6, MP.7, MP.8

**14-2**   **Defining and Non-Defining Attributes of 2-D Shapes** . . . . . . . . . . . . 753
I.G.A.1, MP.3, MP.5, MP.8

**14-3**   **Build and Draw 2-D Shapes by Attributes**. . . . . . . . . . . . . . . . . . . . . 759
I.G.A.1, MP.2, MP.4, MP.5, MP.8

**14-4**   **Compose 2-D Shapes**. . . . . . . . . . . . . . . . . . . . . . . . . . . . . . . . . . . . . 765
I.G.A.2, MP.1, MP.4, MP.7

**14-5**   **Compose New 2-D Shapes from 2-D Shapes** . . . . . . . . . . . . . . . . . . 771
I.G.A.2, MP.1, MP.2, MP.3, MP.4

**14-6**   **Use Attributes to Define Three-Dimensional (3-D) Shapes** . . . . . . . . . 777
I.G.A.1, MP.2, MP.3, MP.8

**14-7**   **Defining and Non-Defining Attributes of 3-D Shapes** . . . . . . . . . . . . 783
I.G.A.1, MP.3, MP.7, MP.8

**14-8**   **Compose with 3-D Shapes** . . . . . . . . . . . . . . . . . . . . . . . . . . . . . . . . 789
I.G.A.2, MP.1, MP.2, MP.6, MP.8

**14-9**   **MATH PRACTICES AND PROBLEM SOLVING**
**Make Sense and Persevere**
MP.1 Also MP.2, MP.6, MP.8, I.G.A.1, I.G.A.2. . . . . . . . . . . . . . . . . . . . 795

Fluency Practice Activity. . . . . . . . . . . . . . . . . . . . . . . . . . . . . . . . . . . . . . . . . 801
Vocabulary Review. . . . . . . . . . . . . . . . . . . . . . . . . . . . . . . . . . . . . . . . . . . . . 802
Reteaching . . . . . . . . . . . . . . . . . . . . . . . . . . . . . . . . . . . . . . . . . . . . . . . . . . . 803
Topic Assessment . . . . . . . . . . . . . . . . . . . . . . . . . . . . . . . . . . . . . . . . . . . . . 807
Topic Performance Assessment. . . . . . . . . . . . . . . . . . . . . . . . . . . . . . . . . . . 811

© Pearson Education, Inc. 1

This circle is divided into quarters.

# TOPIC 15
## Equal Shares of Circles and Rectangles

Math and Science Project. . . . . . . . . . . . . . . . . . . . . . . . . . . . . . . . . . . . . . . 813
Review What You Know. . . . . . . . . . . . . . . . . . . . . . . . . . . . . . . . . . . . . . . 814
Vocabulary Cards. . . . . . . . . . . . . . . . . . . . . . . . . . . . . . . . . . . . . . . . . . . . 815

**15-1** **Make Equal Shares** . . . . . . . . . . . . . . . . . . . . . . . . . . . . . . 817
I.G.A.3, MP.1, MP.4, MP.6, MP.7

**15-2** **Make Halves and Fourths of Rectangles and Circles** . . . . . . . . . . . . 823
I.G.A.3, MP.2, MP.3, MP.6, MP.8

**15-3** **Understand Halves and Fourths.** . . . . . . . . . . . . . . . . . . . . 829
I.G.A.3, MP.2, MP.4, MP.5

**15-4** **MATH PRACTICES AND PROBLEM SOLVING**
**Model with Math**
MP.4 Also MP.2, MP.3, I.G.A.3. . . . . . . . . . . . . . . . . . . . . . . . . . 835

Fluency Practice Activity. . . . . . . . . . . . . . . . . . . . . . . . . . . . . . . . . . . . . . 841
Vocabulary Review. . . . . . . . . . . . . . . . . . . . . . . . . . . . . . . . . . . . . . . . . . 842
Reteaching . . . . . . . . . . . . . . . . . . . . . . . . . . . . . . . . . . . . . . . . . . . . . . . 843
Topic Assessment . . . . . . . . . . . . . . . . . . . . . . . . . . . . . . . . . . . . . . . . . . 845
Topic Performance Assessment. . . . . . . . . . . . . . . . . . . . . . . . . . . . . . . . . 847

PearsonRealize.com

# STEP UP to Grade 2

STEP UP Lessons Opener . . . . . . . . . . . . . . . . . . . . . . . . . . . . . . . . . . . . . . . 849

**SU1** Even and Odd Numbers
2.OA.C.3, 2.OA.B.2, MP.4, MP.5, MP.6, MP.7 . . . . . . . . . . . . . . . . . . . . 851

**SU2** Use Arrays to Find Totals . . . . . . . . . . . . . . . . . . . . . . . . . . 855
2.OA.C.4, 2.OA.B.2, MP.1, MP.3, MP.4, MP.7

**SU3** Add on a Hundred Chart . . . . . . . . . . . . . . . . . . . . . . . . . . . 859
2.NBT.B.5, 2.NBT.B.9, MP.4, MP.7, MP.8

**SU4** Models to Add 2-Digit Numbers . . . . . . . . . . . . . . . . . . . . . . 863
2.NBT.B.5, 2.NBT.B.9, MP.4, MP.5, MP.6

**SU5** Subtract on a Hundred Chart . . . . . . . . . . . . . . . . . . . . . . . . 867
2.NBT.B.5, 2.NBT.B.9, MP.2, MP.4, MP.7, MP.8

**SU6** Models to Subtract 2- and 1-Digit Numbers . . . . . . . . . . . . . 871
2.NBT.B.5, 2.NBT.B.9, MP.2, MP.3, MP.4, MP.5

**SU7** Tell Time to Five Minutes . . . . . . . . . . . . . . . . . . . . . . . . . . . 875
2.MD.C.7, 2.NBT.A.2, MP.2, MP.5, MP.6, MP.8

**SU8** Understand Hundreds . . . . . . . . . . . . . . . . . . . . . . . . . . . . . 879
2.NBT.A.1a, 2.NBT.A.1b, MP.2, MP.4, MP.5, MP.7

**SU9** Counting Hundreds, Tens, and Ones . . . . . . . . . . . . . . . . . . . 883
2.NBT.A.1, MP.2, MP.4, MP.7

**SU10** Skip Count by 5, 10, and 100, to 1,000 . . . . . . . . . . . . . . . . . 887
2.NBT.A.2, MP.2, MP.4, MP.7, MP.8

Glossary . . . . . . . . . . . . . . . . . . . . . . . . . . . . . . . . . . . . . . . . . . . . . . . . . . . . G1

These lessons help prepare you for Grade 2.

Contents

Math practices are ways we think about and do math.

Math practices will help you solve problems.

# Math Practices

**MP.1** Make sense of problems and persevere in solving them.

**MP.2** Reason abstractly and quantitatively.

**MP.3** Construct viable arguments and critique the reasoning of others.

**MP.4** Model with mathematics.

**MP.5** Use appropriate tools strategically.

**MP.6** Attend to precision.

**MP.7** Look for and make use of structure.

**MP.8** Look for and express regularity in repeated reasoning.

There are good Thinking Habits for each of these math practices.

## MP.1 Make sense of problems and persevere in solving them.

My plan was to find all the ways 9 counters can be put into 2 groups.

Good math thinkers know what the problem is about. They have a plan to solve it. They keep trying if they get stuck.

What pairs of numbers from 0 to 9 add to 9?

$0 + 9 = 9$
$1 + 8 = 9$
$2 + 7 = 9$

### Thinking Habits

What do I need to find?

What do I know?

What's my plan for solving the problem?

What else can I try if I get stuck?

How can I check that my solution makes sense?

## MP.2 Reason abstractly and quantitatively.

I thought about what numbers would make 8. I used an equation with those numbers to show the problem.

Good math thinkers know how to think about words and numbers to solve problems.

Alan has 8 blue marbles.
He wants to give them to Tom and Rosi.
How can Alan break apart the
8 blue marbles?

Tom               Rosi

$8 = 3 + 5$

## Thinking Habits

What do the numbers stand for?

How are the numbers in the problem related?

How can I show a word problem using pictures or numbers?

How can I use a word problem to show what an equation means?

Math Practices and Problem Solving Handboo

## MP.3 Construct viable arguments and critique the reasoning of others.

I used a picture and words to explain my thinking.

Good math thinkers use math to explain why they are right. They talk about math that others do, too.

Joan has 7 pencils. Sam has 9 pencils.
Who has more pencils? Show how you know.

I drew pencils for Joan and for Sam. I matched up the pencils. Sam has more pencils than Joan.

Joan's pencils

Sam's pencils

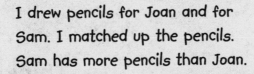

### Thinking Habits

How can I use math to explain my work?

Am I using numbers and symbols correctly?

Is my explanation clear?

What questions can I ask to understand other people's thinking?

Are there mistakes in other people's thinking?

Can I improve other people's thinking?

I used ten-frames to show the problem.

Good math thinkers use math they know to show and solve problems.

Ali collects rocks. He puts 17 rocks in boxes. Each box holds 10 rocks. He fills 1 box. How many rocks are in the second box?

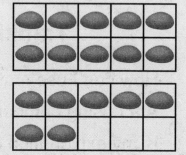

## Thinking Habits

How can I use the math I know to help solve this problem?

Can I use a drawing, diagram, table, graph, or objects to show the problem?

Can I write an equation to show the problem?

**MP.5** Use appropriate tools strategically.

I chose to use cubes to solve the problem.

Good math thinkers know how to pick the right tools to solve math problems.

Ed finds 5 nuts on a tree. He finds 4 more nuts in the grass. How many nuts does Ed find?

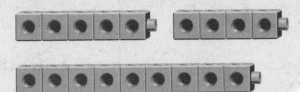

## Thinking Habits

Which tools can I use?

Is there a different tool I could use?

Am I using the tool correctly?

## MP.6  Attend to precision.

Good math thinkers are careful about what they write and say, so their ideas about math are clear.

I used math words correctly to write what I noticed.

How are these shapes alike?

They have 4 sides.
They have 4 corners.
They have straight sides.

## Thinking Habits

Am I using numbers, units, and symbols correctly?

Am I using the correct definitions?

Is my answer clear?

**Math Practices and Problem Solving Handbook**

Good math thinkers look for patterns in math to help solve problems.

I found a pattern.

What are the next two numbers? Fill in the blanks. Explain and show your thinking.

15, 16, 17, 18, 19, _____, _____

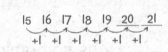

15  16  17  18  19  20  21
  +1  +1  +1  +1  +1  +1

## Thinking Habits

Is there a pattern?

How can I describe the pattern?

Can I break the problem into simpler parts?

## MP.8 Look for and express regularity in repeated reasoning.

Each new person has 1 more box. I used what I know about counting on to solve this problem.

Good math thinkers look for things that repeat in a problem. They use what they learn from one problem to help them solve other problems.

Jay has 3 boxes.
Nicole has 1 more box than Jay.
Krista has 1 more box than Nicole.
How many boxes does Nicole have?
How many boxes does Krista have? Explain.

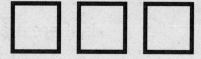

1 more than 3 is 4.
Nicole has 4 boxes.
1 more than 4 is 5.
Krista has 5 boxes.

### Thinking Habits

Does something repeat in the problem?

How can the solution help me solve another problem?

**Math Practices and Problem Solving Handbook**

# Problem Solving Guide

Math practices can help you solve problems.

## Make Sense of the Problem

### Reason
- What do I need to find?
- What given information can I use?
- How are the quantities related?

### Think About Similar Problems
- Have I solved problems like this before?

## Persevere in Solving the Problem

### Model with Math
- How can I use the math I know?
- How can I show the problem?
- Is there a pattern I can use?

### Use Appropriate Tools
- What math tools could I use?
- How can I use those tools?

## Check the Answer

### Make Sense of the Answer
- Is my answer reasonable?

### Check for Precision
- Did I check my work?
- Is my answer clear?
- Is my explanation clear?

### Some Ways to Show Problems
- Draw a Picture
- Draw a Number Line
- Write an Equation

### Some Math Tools
- Objects
- Technology
- Paper and Pencil

**Math Practices and Problem Solving Handbook**

# Problem Solving Recording Sheet

This sheet helps you organize your work.

---

Name **Ehrin**

Teaching Tool **1**

## Problem Solving Recording Sheet

**Problem:**
Billy has 8 green marbles and 4 blue marbles.
How many marbles does he have in all?

Make 10 to solve.
Show your work.

### MAKE SENSE OF THE PROBLEM

| Need to Find | Given |
|---|---|
| I need to find how many marbles Billy has in all. | Billy has 8 green marbles and 4 blue marbles. |

### PERSEVERE IN SOLVING THE PROBLEM

**Some Ways to Represent Problems**
☑ Draw a Picture
☐ Draw a Number Line
☑ Write an Equation

**Some Math Tools**
☐ Objects
☐ Technology
☑ Paper and Pencil

**Solution and Answer**

10                         2

$$8 + 2 = 10$$
$$10 + 2 = 12$$
Billy has 12 marbles.

### CHECK THE ANSWER

I counted the counters I drew.
There are 12.
My answer is correct.

TT1

# Understand Place Value

**Essential Question:** How can you count and add using tens and ones?

There is more daylight during the summer than there is during the winter.

Wow! Let's do this project and learn more.

## Math and Science Project: Daylight Throughout the Year

**Find Out** Talk to friends and relatives about why there is more daylight in summer than in winter. Ask them to help you find information about the changes in daylight each season.

**Journal: Make a Book** Draw pictures of the tilting globe and the sun at different times of the year. In your book, also:

• Add labels to show summer and winter.

• Write a sentence to describe the pattern of the seasons in your own words.

Name _____

# Review What You Know

## A-Z Vocabulary

**1.** Circle the **tens digit**.

48

**2.** Circle the **ones digit**.

76

**3.** Use the **ten-frames** to find the sum.

$7 + 9 =$ _____

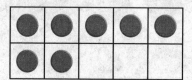
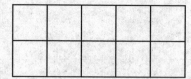

## Counting to 120

**4.** Write the number that comes next when counting forward by 1s. Use a hundred chart to help you.

110, 111, 112, _____

**5.** Maria counts by 10s. She starts at 30. Write the missing numbers.

30, _____, _____,

60, _____

## Hundred Chart

**6.** Write the missing numbers in this part of the hundred chart.

| 42 |    | 44 |    | 46 |
|----|----|----|----|----|
|    | 53 | 54 |    |    |

Name _____

Help  Tools  Games

**Another Look!** Each number 11 through 19 has 1 ten and some ones.

Write the number of ones for each number.
Then write the number word.

**HOME ACTIVITY** Write the numbers 11 through 19 on separate index cards. Show one card to your child. Ask him or her to write the number of tens and ones in the number on the other side of the card. Then ask him or her to write the name for the number. After you have worked through all the cards, you will have a set of flashcards that you and your child can save and use for additional practice.

| 12 | 16 | 11 |
|---|---|---|
| 1 ten and <u>2</u> ones | 1 ten and <u>6</u> ones | 1 ten and <u>1</u> one |
| <u>twelve</u> | <u>sixteen</u> | <u>eleven</u> |

Write the missing words or numbers.

1. _____

☐ 14 is 1 ten and 4 ones.

2. fifteen

☐ is 1 ten and 5 ones.

3. nineteen

☐ is 1 ten and 9 ones.

4. thirteen

☐ 13 is 1 ten and 3 _____.

Write the missing words or numbers.

**5.** _____

$\boxed{17}$ is 1 ten and 7 ones.

**6.** eighteen

$\boxed{18}$ is 1 _____ and 8 ones.

**7. Algebra** $10 + \underline{\phantom{00}} = 16$

**8. Algebra** $12 = \underline{\phantom{00}} + 2$

**9. Higher Order Thinking** Choose a number from 15 through 19. Draw a picture to show how to make the number with ten-frames. Write the number and the number word.

number: _____

number word: _____

**10. © Assessment** Match the numbers on the left with the number word on the right.

| | |
|---|---|
| 10 and 9 | thirteen |
| 1 ten and 0 ones | nineteen |
| 1 ten and 2 ones | eleven |
| 10 and 3 | ten |
| 1 ten and 1 one | twelve |

© Pearson Education, Inc. 1

Name _____

**Another Look!** You can count to quickly add tens.

The tens digit tells how many groups of 10 there are!

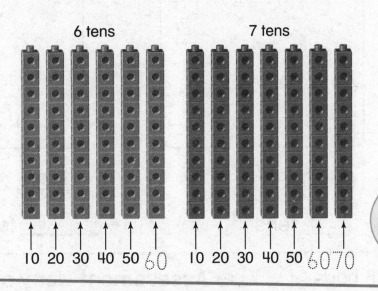

6 tens          7 tens

10 20 30 40 50 60     10 20 30 40 50 6070

There are no extra cubes. So the ones digit is always 0!

**HOME ACTIVITY** Say a number of tens (from I ten to 9 tens) and ask your child to tell you how many that is in all. For example, 2 tens is 20.

Count to find how many tens.

**1.**

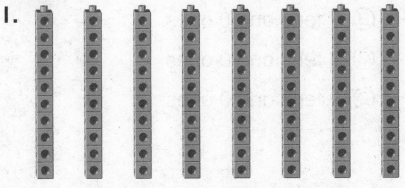

____, ____, ____, ____, ____, ____, ____, ____

____ tens and ____ ones

**2.**

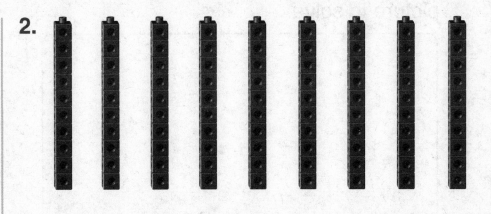

____, ____, ____, ____, ____, ____, ____, ____, ____

____ tens and ____ ones

Draw the cubes for the counting shown. Then write the total.

**3.**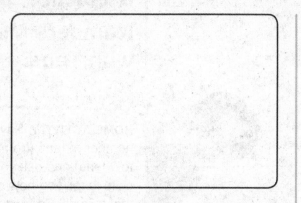

10, 20, 30, 40, 50, 60, 70

_____ tens

**4.**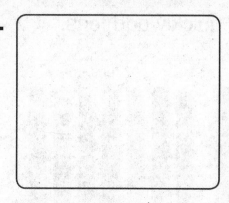

10, 20, 30

_____ tens

**5.**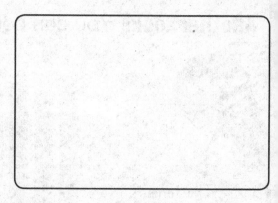

10, 20, 30, 40, 50, 60

_____ tens

**6. Higher Order Thinking** May has 5 bags. Each bag has 10 marbles in it. There are no marbles outside the bags. How many marbles does May have in all? Draw a picture to solve.

May has _____ marbles.

**7. ◎ Assessment** Jerry buys a notebook that has 90 pages. Which of the following can represent 90 pages?

Ⓐ 6 tens and 0 ones

Ⓑ 7 tens and 0 ones

Ⓒ 8 tens and 0 ones

Ⓓ 9 tens and 0 ones

Name _____

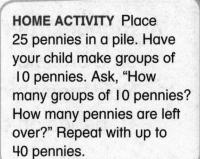

**Another Look!** You can count by 10s and then the leftover 1s.

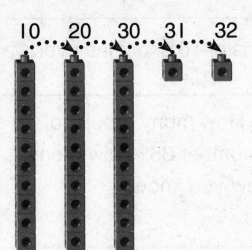

10   20   30   31   32

3 groups of 10   2 left over

32 in all

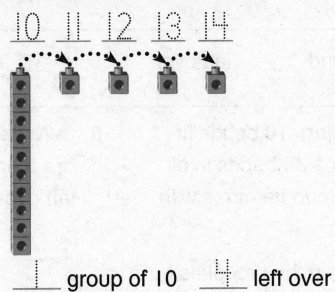

10  11  12  13  14

___1___ group of 10   ___4___ left over

___14___ in all

**HOME ACTIVITY** Place 25 pennies in a pile. Have your child make groups of 10 pennies. Ask, "How many groups of 10 pennies? How many pennies are left over?" Repeat with up to 40 pennies.

Count by 10s and 1s. Write the numbers.

1. _____  _____  _____  _____

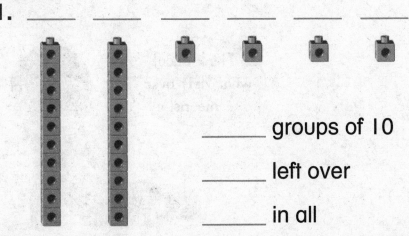

_____ groups of 10

_____ left over

_____ in all

2. _____  _____  _____  _____

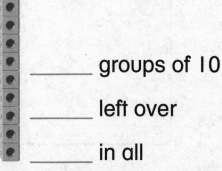

_____ groups of 10

_____ left over

_____ in all

Write the missing number.

**3.** _____ is 1 group of 10 and 2 left over.

**4.** 31 is _____ groups of 10 and 1 left over.

**5.** 14 is 1 group of 10 and _____ left over.

**6.** _____ is 2 groups of 10 and 7 left over.

**7. Higher Order Thinking** 10 beads fit on a bracelet. Ben has 34 beads in all. How many bracelets can he make with 10 beads on each?

Draw a picture to show the bracelets he can make with his beads. Then draw the beads that will be left over.

**8. © Assessment** How many groups of 10 are there in the number 38? How many left over? Tell how you know.

_____

_____

_____

_____

Think about what "left over" means.

Name _____

**Another Look!** You can use a workmat to show tens and ones.

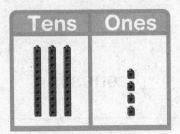

| Tens | Ones |
|------|------|

3 tens is 30.

4 ones is 4.

3 tens and 4 ones is 34.

| Tens | Ones |
|------|------|

I ten is __10__ .

3 ones is __3__ .

__1__ ten and __3__ ones is __13__ .

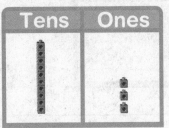
Think about the number of tens and ones.

**HOME ACTIVITY** Draw 2 squares side by side. Write a 3 in the left square and label it "Tens." Write a 4 in the right square and label it "Ones." Have your child draw a picture to show the number. Ask him or her to use the terms *ones* and *tens* to describe how many.

Count the tens and ones. Then write the numbers.

**I.**

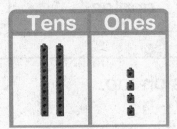

| Tens | Ones |
|------|------|

_____ tens is _____ .

_____ ones is _____ .

_____ tens and _____ ones is _____ .

**2.**

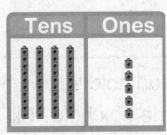

| Tens | Ones |
|------|------|

_____ tens is _____ .

_____ ones is _____ .

_____ tens and _____ ones is _____ .

Count the tens and ones. Then write the numbers.

3.
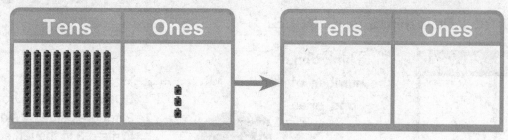

| Tens | Ones |
| --- | --- |
|  |  |

_____ tens and _____ ones is _____.

4. Write the missing number.

6 tens and _____ ones is the same as 60.

5. **Higher Order Thinking** Sara buys 4 boxes of apples. There are 10 apples in each box. She also buys one bag with 8 apples. How many apples does Sara buy?

Draw a picture to solve the questions.

Sara bought _____ apples

6. © **Assessment** A box can hold 4 rows of 10 movies and 2 extra movies on top. How many movies can the box hold? Fill in the missing numbers.

_____ tens and _____ ones is _____.

_____ movies

Name _____

**Another Look!** You can show the tens and ones in a number by drawing a picture.

How many tens and ones are in 56?

I count by 10s to 50.
I draw a line for each number I say.
I draw 5 lines.

Then I count by 1s from 50 to 56.
I draw a dot for each number I say.
I draw 6 dots.

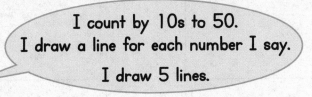

10  20  30  40  50  51  52  53  54  55  56

There are __5__ tens and __6__ ones in 56.

**HOME ACTIVITY** Give your child a number between 0 and 99 and ask him or her to draw a model to represent it. When the model is drawn, ask your child to count by 10s and 1s to show you that the model correctly represents the number. Make sure that he or she points to one line each time when counting by tens and to one dot each time when counting by ones. Repeat with other numbers.

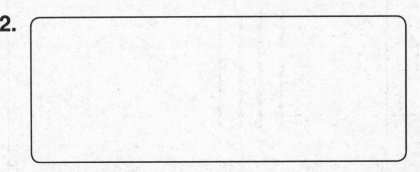

Draw models to help you find the number of tens and ones in each number.

1.

There are _____ tens and _____ ones in 72.

2.

There are _____ tens and _____ ones in 43.

Draw models to help you find the number of tens and ones in each number.

**3.**

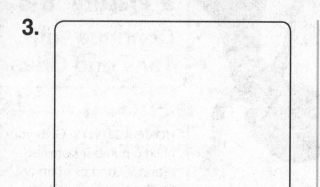

There are _____ tens and _____ ones in 58.

**4.**

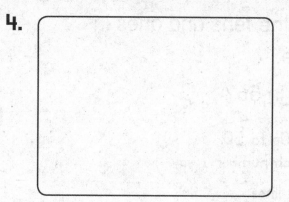

There are _____ tens and _____ ones in 7.

**5.**

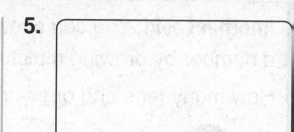

There are _____ tens and _____ ones in 90.

**6. Higher Order Thinking** Haley starts drawing a model for the number 84, but she gets interrupted. Help her finish her model.

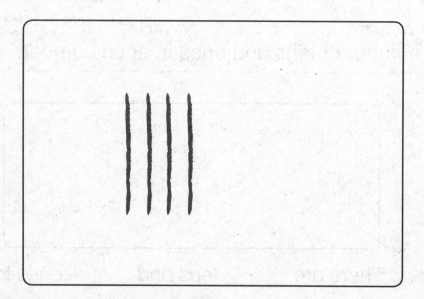

**7. © Assessment** Which number is represented here?

Ⓐ 15

Ⓑ 11

Ⓒ 50

Ⓓ 51

© Pearson Education, Inc. 1

Name _____

**Another Look!** You can make a list to solve problems.

What are all the ways you can show 49 as tens and ones?

| Tens | Ones |
|------|------|
| 4 | 9 |
| 3 | 19 |
| 2 | 29 |
| 1 | 39 |
| 0 | 49 |

Making a list can help you see the pattern and make sure you find all the ways.

Make a list to solve each problem. You can use cubes to help you.

1. Mark wants to show 34 as tens and ones. What are all the ways?

| Tens | Ones |
|------|------|
|  |  |
|  |  |
|  |  |
|  |  |

2. Maya wants to show 28 as tens and ones. What are all the ways?

| Tens | Ones |
|------|------|
|  |  |
|  |  |
|  |  |

**Flowers** Zach has 53 flowers to plant. He wants to plant them in groups of 10s and 1s. Zach can plant 10 flowers in each flower box. He can plant 1 flower in each pot.

How many different ways can Zach plant flowers in boxes and pots?

**Zach's List**

| Boxes | Pots |
|-------|------|
| 5 | 3 |
| 4 | 13 |
| 3 | 23 |
| 2 | 33 |
| 1 | 43 |

3. **MP.2 Reasoning** Zach listed the ways he could plant the flowers. Did he list all possible ways? Tell how you know. If Zach missed any ways, list them below.

4. **MP.3 Explain** Zach only wants to plant a group of ten flowers in each box. Is there any way that Zach could plant all 53 flowers using only boxes? Explain how you know.

5. **MP.7 Look for Patterns** How many ways can Zach plant the flowers in boxes and pots? How can you use a pattern to check that you have found all the ways?

Name _____

**Point & Tally**

Find a partner. Get paper and a pencil.

Each partner chooses a different color: light blue or dark blue.

Partner 1 and Partner 2 each point to a black number at the same time. Both partners add those numbers.

If the answer is on your color, you get a tally mark.

Work until one partner gets twelve tally marks.

**I can ...**
add and subtract within 10.

© Content Standard 1.OA.C.6

| Partner 1 | | | | | | | Partner 2 |
|---|---|---|---|---|---|---|---|
| **5** | 7 | 6 | 10 | 9 | 8 | 1 | **4** |
| **4** | | | | | | | **3** |
| **1** | | | | | | | **5** |
| **3** | 2 | 3 | 0 | 4 | 3 | 5 | **1** |
| **2** | | | | | | | **3** |
| **1** | | | | | | | **2** |

| Tally Marks for Partner 1 | Tally Marks for Partner 2 |
|---|---|
| | |

Glossary

**Word List**
- fewer
- more
- ones
- tens

## Understand Vocabulary

1. Write the number word that is one more than fourteen.

_____

2. Write the number word that is one fewer than eighteen.

_____

3. Circle the cubes that make 2 tens.

4. Circle the cubes that make 1 ten and 5 ones.

5. Circle the cubes that make 3 tens and 3 ones.

## Use Vocabulary in Writing

6. Write a story problem for a number between 11 and 19. Then solve by using words from the Word List. Show your work.

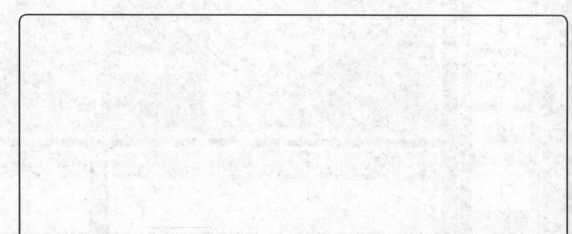

Name _____

## Set A

You can group objects by 10 to count.

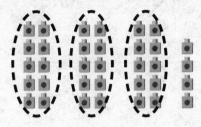

__34__ is __3__ groups of 10

and __4__ ones left over.

Circle groups of 10.
Write the numbers.

1.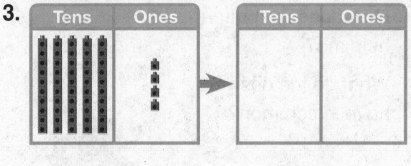

_____ is _____ groups of 10
and _____ ones left over.

2.

_____ is _____ group of 10
and _____ ones left over.

## Set B

You can show a two-digit number as tens and ones.

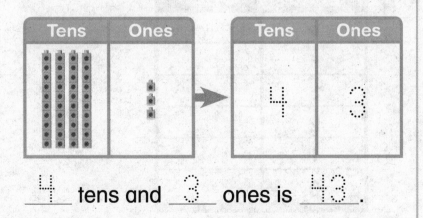

| Tens | Ones |
| --- | --- |
| | |

| Tens | Ones |
| --- | --- |
| 4 | 3 |

__4__ tens and __3__ ones is __43__.

Count the tens and ones.
Then write the number.

3.

| Tens | Ones |
| --- | --- |
| | |

| Tens | Ones |
| --- | --- |
| | |

_____ tens and _____ ones is _____.

You can draw a model to show tens and ones.

There are __3__ tens and __6__ ones in 36.

**Draw a model to show tens and ones.**

4. There are _____ tens and _____ ones in 78.

## Thinking Habits

**Look For and Use Structure**

Is there a pattern to the answers?

How does the pattern help me?

What do the answers have in common?

**Use patterns and make a list to solve.**

5. Lupita wants to show 54 as tens and ones. What are all the ways?

54

| Tens | Ones |
|------|------|
| 5 | |
| 4 | |
| 3 | |
| 2 | |
| 1 | |
| 0 | |

© Pearson Education, Inc. 1

Digital Resources

Solve  Learn  Glossary

Tools  Assessment  Help  Games

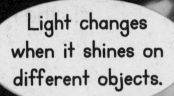

Light changes when it shines on different objects.

When light shines on stained glass, the light that passes through is the same color as the glass.

Wow! Let's do this project and learn more.

## Math and Science Project: Light and Objects

**Find Out** Talk to friends and relatives about light. Discuss how light changes when it shines on different kinds of objects.

**Journal: Make a Book** Show what you found out. In your book, also:

- Draw pictures showing light shining on objects that are see-through and not see-through.

- Make up and solve number stories about shining light on different objects.

Name _____

## A-Z Vocabulary

**1.** Circle the group of cubes that has **more**.

**2.** Circle the group of cubes that has **less**.

**3.** How many **tens** are in the number?

50

_____ tens

## Number Lines

**4.** Use the number line to count by 10s. Write the missing numbers.

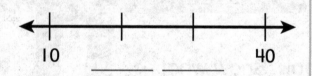

10                    40

_____  _____

## Hundred Chart

**6.** Use the part of the hundred chart to count.

| 11 | 12 | 13 | 14 | 15 | 16 | 17 | 18 | 19 | 20 |
|----|----|----|----|----|----|----|----|----|----|
| 21 | 22 | 23 | 24 | 25 | 26 | 27 | 28 | 29 | 30 |
| 31 | 32 | 33 | 34 | 35 | 36 | 37 | 38 | 39 | 40 |

18, 19, _____, _____, _____

**5.** Pat sees 5 bugs. Erin sees 6 bugs. How many bugs did they see in all?

Use the number line to count.

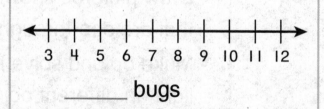

3  4  5  6  7  8  9  10  11  12

_____ bugs

© Pearson Education, Inc. 1

Name _____

Help  Tools  Games

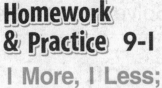
**Another Look!** You can use place-value blocks to show
1 more than, 1 less than, 10 more than, or 10 less than.

34

You can cross out 1 cube
to show 1 less than 34.

1 less than 34 is ___33___.

You can add 1 more cube
to show 1 more than 34.

1 more than 34 is ___35___.

You can cross out 1 ten
to show 10 less than 34.

10 less than 34 is ___24___.

You can add 1 more ten
to show 10 more than 34.

10 more than 34 is ___44___.

**HOME ACTIVITY** Write a
two-digit number. Have your
child write the numbers
that are 1 more than, 1 less
than, 10 more than, and
10 less than the number.
Provide pennies as counters
if needed. Continue with
several two-digit numbers.

Complete each sentence.

1.

1 more than 23 is _____.

1 less than 23 is _____.

2.

10 less than 68 is _____.

10 more than 68 is _____.

Solve each problem below. You can draw pictures to help you.

3. 24

1 more than 24 is _____.

1 less than 24 is _____.

10 more than 24 is _____.

10 less than 24 is _____.

4. 67

1 more than 67 is _____.

1 less than 67 is _____.

10 more than 67 is _____.

10 less than 67 is _____.

5. **Higher Order Thinking** Follow the arrows. Write the number that is 1 more, 1 less; 10 more, or 10 less.

You can draw pictures to help you.

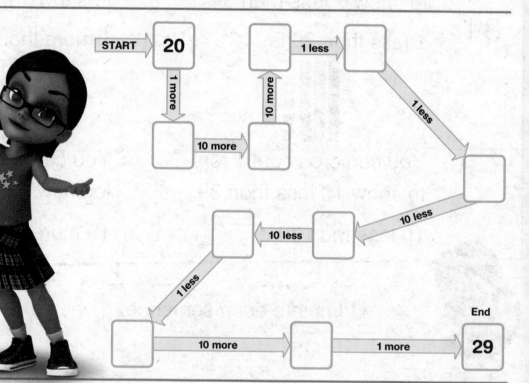

START → 20

1 more ↓ · 10 more ↑ · 1 less → · 1 less

10 more → · 10 less ← · 10 less

1 less ↓ · 10 more → · 1 more → End 29

6. © **Assessment**

Match each number with its description.

23     1     13     55

10 more than 3    1 more than 54    10 less than 33    1 less than 2

© Pearson Education, Inc. 1

**Topic 9** | Lesson 1

Name _____

**Another Look!** You can use a hundred chart to find 1 more, 1 less, 10 more, or 10 less than a number.

| 1 | 2 | 3 | 4 | 5 |
|---|---|---|---|---|
| 11 | 12 | 13 | 14 | 15 |
| 21 | 22 | 23 | 24 | 25 |
| 31 | 32 | 33 | 34 | 35 |
| 41 | 42 | 43 | 44 | 45 |

What is 1 more, 1 less, 10 more, and 10 less than 23?

Look at the number in the space after 23 to find 1 more.

1 more than 23 is ___24___.

Look at the number in the space before 23 to find 1 less.

1 less than 23 is ___22___.

Look at the number 1 row below 23 to find 10 more.

10 more than 23 is ___33___.

Look at the number 1 row above 23 to find 10 less.

10 less than 23 is ___13___.

**HOME ACTIVITY** Write a number between 11 and 89 on a sheet of paper. Have your child write the number that is 1 more, 1 less, 10 more, and 10 less than the number. Repeat with several other numbers. Discuss the patterns your child notices.

Use a hundred chart to complete each sentence.

1. 1 more than 77 is _____.

   1 less than 77 is _____.

   10 more than 77 is _____.

   10 less than 77 is _____.

2. 1 more than 62 is _____.

   1 less than 62 is _____.

   10 more than 62 is _____.

   10 less than 62 is _____.

3. 1 more than 89 is _____.

   1 less than 89 is _____.

   10 more than 89 is _____.

   10 less than 89 is _____.

Complete the part of the hundred chart to find 1 more, 1 less, 10 more, or 10 less.

4.

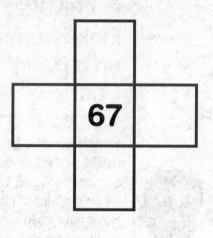

5.

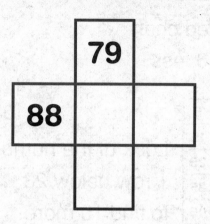

6.

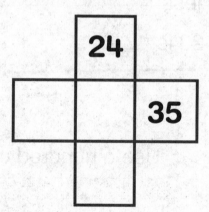

7. **Higher Order Thinking** How can you use place-value blocks and a hundred chart to show the number that is 10 more than 43? What is the number?

8. © **Assessment** Complete the part of the number chart by finding 1 more, 1 less, 10 more, or 10 less.

© Pearson Education, Inc. 1

**Topic 9** | Lesson 2

Name _____

Help   Tools   Games

**Another Look!** You can compare numbers to decide if one number is greater than or less than another number.

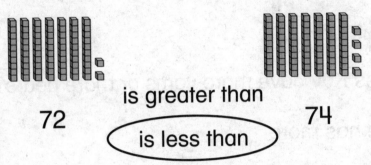

72   is greater than / (is less than)

74   29   (is greater than) / is less than   25.

**HOME ACTIVITY** Give your child 2 two-digit numbers. Have him or her finish one of these sentences: ____ is greater than ____ or ____ is less than ____. If needed, have your child draw pictures to solve. Consider using numbers where the tens digit or ones digit is the same. This allows him or her to compare only the tens or ones digit to determine which is greater or less.

 Write a number to match each model. Then circle **is greater than** or **is less than**.

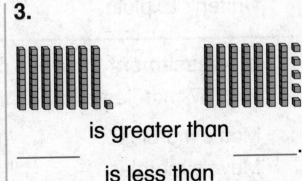

**1.** _____ is greater than / is less than _____.

**2.** _____ is greater than / is less than _____.

**3.** _____ is greater than / is less than _____.

Topic 9 | Lesson 3

Digital Resources at PearsonRealize.com

five hundred thirteen **513**

Solve each problem below. Then complete each sentence.

4. Ty counts 29 fish at the zoo.
   He counts 22 birds at the zoo.

   Did Ty count more birds or more fish?

   He counted more _____.

   _____ is greater than _____.

5. Kay has 18 yams.
   She has 21 pears.

   Does Kay have more yams or more pears?

   She has more _____.

   _____ is less than _____.

6. **Higher Order Thinking** Adam writes a number. The number is greater than 50 and less than 54. What numbers could Adam have written? Explain.

   _____

   _____

   _____

7. © **Assessment** Matt has more than 41 marbles and less than 43 marbles. Maya has more than 47 marbles and less than 49 marbles. Draw lines to each statement to make it true.

   Matt's marbles        40
   Maya's marbles        42
                         48
                         50

   Matt has _____ marbles than Maya.        more
                                                fewer

© Pearson Education, Inc. 1

Name _____

**Another Look!** You can use < to show that a number is less than another number.

You can use > to show that a number is greater than another number.

You can use = to show that a number is equal to another number.

**HOME ACTIVITY** Write 2 two-digit numbers. Leave space between the numbers. Have your child write <, >, or = to compare the numbers. Then have him or her read the sentence, replacing the symbol with "is greater than," "is less than," or "is equal to." Repeat with other numbers.

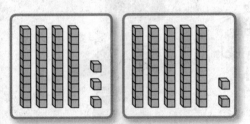

43  52

43 is less than 52.

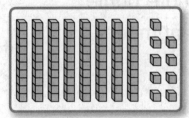

89  75

89 is _greater than_ 75.

 Write >, <, or = to complete the sentence.
Then write **greater than, less than,** or **equal to**.

1.
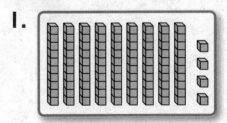

94 ◯ 95

94 is _____ 95

2.

31 ◯ 31

31 is _____ 31

Write >, <, or = to compare the numbers.

3. 45 ◯ 50 | 4. 97 ◯ 97 | 5. 21 ◯ 12 | 6. 33 ◯ 63

7. © **MP.6 Be Precise** Brandon has 79 bottle caps. Gemma has 88 bottle caps. Who has more bottle caps? Write >, <, or = to compare the numbers. Then solve the problem.

Remember to use symbols correctly!

_____ ◯ _____

_____ has more bottle caps.

8. **Higher Order Thinking** Choose 2 numbers. Write 2 different sentences to compare the numbers. Use **is greater than, is less than**, or **is equal to.** Then use >, <, or = .

_____

_____

_____

9. © **Assessment** Ginny wrote these four equations for class. Which of Ginny's sentences are **NOT** true? Choose all that apply.

☐ 62 < 27

☐ 18 > 24

☐ 42 < 52

☐ 17 = 71

Name _____

  Help Tools Games

**Another Look!** You can use a number line to compare numbers.

Find a number that is less than 64 and a number that is greater than 64.

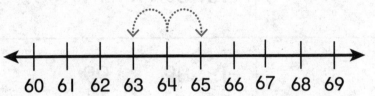

60  61  62  63  64  65  66  67  68  69

On a number line, numbers to the left are less and numbers to the right are greater!

_63_ < 64          _65_ > 64

_63_ is less than 64.          _65_ is greater than 64.

Write the number or symbol > or < to make each correct. Use the number line to help you.

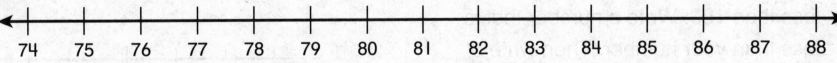

74  75  76  77  78  79  80  81  82  83  84  85  86  87  88

1. _____ < 84          2. 82 > _____          3. 78 < _____

4. 84 ◯ 88          5. 76 ◯ 75          6. 74 ◯ 81

Write > or < to make each correct. Draw a number line to help you if you wish.

7. 29 ◯ 42

8. 63 ◯ 71

9. 34 ◯ 28

10. 47 ◯ 53

11. 87 ◯ 76

12. 39 ◯ 14

13. 77 ◯ 63

14. 24 ◯ 34

15. 89 ◯ 99

16. Andrew is thinking of a number less than 52 and greater than 40. His number has 3 ones. What is Andrew's number?

_____

17. © MP.4 Model  What number is less than 23 and more than 21?

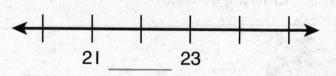

18. **Higher Order Thinking** Choose a number that is greater than 50 and less than 100. Write a number that is less than your number. Then write a number that is greater than your number.

_____ is less than _____.

_____ is greater than _____.

19. © **Assessment**  Which numbers are less than 79? Choose all that apply.

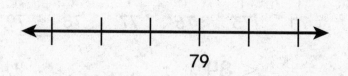

75 ☐          78 ☐          80 ☐          81 ☐

Name _____

Help  Tools  Games

**Another Look!** Making a list can help you make sense of a problem.

I can use the first clue to make a list of what the answer could be.

Then I can use the second clue to make my list even smaller and find the answer.

    **82  55  52  47**

Ian's number is less than 60.
His numbers could be __47__, __52__, and __55__.

Ian says his number has a 2 in the ones place.
Ian's number is __52__.

Make sense of the problems to find the secret numbers from the list below. Show your work.

**48    98    62    92**

1. Ben's number is less than 90.
His numbers could be

_____

Ben's number does **NOT** have a 4 in the tens place.

The number is _____.

2. Tim's number is greater than 50.
His numbers could be

_____

Tim says his number has an 8 in the ones place.

The number is _____.

**Numbers in Shapes** Jeffrey chooses a secret number from the choices at right. He gives clues to help you find it. What is the secret number?

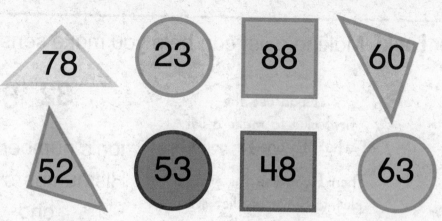

Jeffery's Clues:

- The secret number is **NOT** in a green shape.
- The number has a 3 in the ones place.
- The number is greater than 50.

3. **MP.1 Make Sense** What is your plan for solving this problem?

_____

_____

_____

_____

4. **MP.3 Explain** What is the secret number? How do you know your answer is correct?

_____

_____

_____

_____

_____

_____

**Secret number:** _____

Does your answer fit all the clues?

© Pearson Education, Inc. 1

Name _____

Find a partner. Point to a clue. Read the clue.

Look below the clues to find a match. Write the clue letter in the box next to the match.

Find a match for every clue.

**I can ...**
add and subtract within 10.

© Content Standard 1.OA.C.6

**Clues**

**A** 6 + 2

**B** 5 + 5

**C** 9 − 3

**D** 5 − 1

**E** 8 − 6

**F** 5 + 4

**G** 7 − 2

**H** 1 + 2

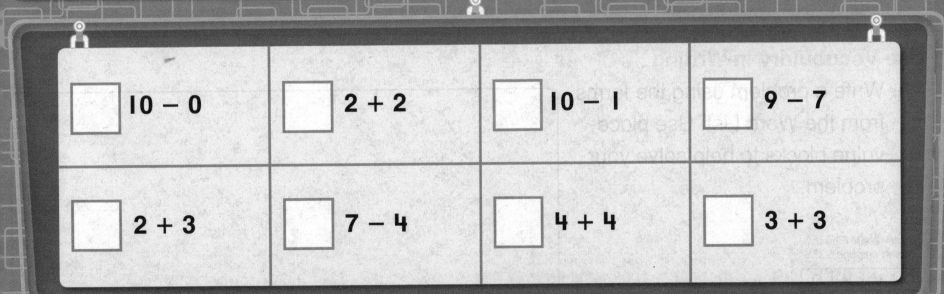

| | | | |
|---|---|---|---|
| ☐ 10 − 0 | ☐ 2 + 2 | ☐ 10 − 1 | ☐ 9 − 7 |
| ☐ 2 + 3 | ☐ 7 − 4 | ☐ 4 + 4 | ☐ 3 + 3 |

*Answers for* Find a Match *on next page.*

A-Z
Glossary

**Word List**
- compare
- greater than ($>$)
- less
- less than ($<$)
- more

## Understand Vocabulary

**1.** Compare the numbers. Circle the number that is more.

26  29

**2.** Compare the numbers. Circle the number that is less.

58  68

**3.** Choose a term from the Word List. Fill in the blank to make it true.

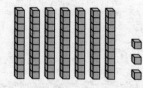 is _____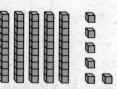

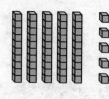 is 10 _____ than

## Use Vocabulary in Writing

**4.** Write a problem using the terms from the Word List. Use place-value blocks to help solve your problem.

*Answers to* Find a Match *on page 533.*

| B | D | F | E |
|---|---|---|---|
| G | H | A | C |

Name _____

**Set A**

You can use blocks to show
I more, I less, 10 more,
and 10 less than a number.

Use blocks. Write the numbers
to complete each sentence.

34

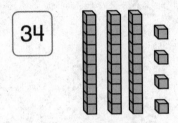

I less than 34 is _33_.

10 more than 34 is _44_.

**I.** 87

I more than 87 is _____.

I less than 87 is _____.

10 more than 87 is _____.

10 less than 87 is _____.

**Set B**

You can use a hundred chart
to find the number that is
I more than, I less than,
10 more than, and 10 less than.

| 35 | 36 | 37 | 38 | 39 |
|----|----|----|----|----|
| 45 | 46 | 47 | **48** | 49 |
| 55 | 56 | 57 | 58 | 59 |

I more than 48 is _49_.

10 less than 48 is _38_.

Write the number that is I more, I less,
10 more, or 10 less. You can use a
hundred chart to help you.

**2.** I less than 37

_____, 37

**3.** I more than 37

37, _____

**4.** 10 less than 55

_____, 55

**5.** 10 more than 55

55, _____

You can compare numbers using >, <, or =.

> means greater than.
33 is greater than 24.

33 ⟩ 24

< means less than.
24 is less than 33.

24 ⟨ 33

Write **greater than**, **less than**, or **equal to**. Then write >, <, or =.

6. 46 is _____ 26.

46 ◯ 26

7. 25 is _____ 52.

25 ◯ 52

**Thinking Habits**

Make Sense and Persevere

What am I asked to find?

What is a good plan for solving this problem?

How can I check that my solution makes sense?

Look at the numbers below.
Find the secret number.

| 42 | 73 | 91 | 7 | 13 | 63 | 50 |

8. I am a number greater than 65.
What numbers could I be?

_____

9. I am 10 less than 83.
What number am I?

_____

Name _____

Help   Tools   Games

**Another Look!** If you know how to add ones, you can add tens.

$$40 + 50 = ?$$

9 tens is 90.
So, $40 + 50 = \underline{90}$.

$40 + 50$ is the same as
4 tens + 5 tens.

4 tens + 5 tens = 9 tens

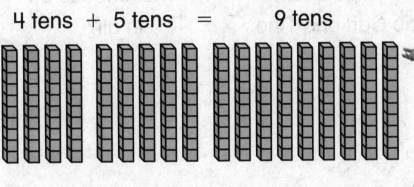

**HOME ACTIVITY** Count by 1s from 1–10 with your child. Then count by 10s together from 10–100. Discuss how these counting sequences are similar. What is the relationship between the numbers you count when you count by 1s and those you count when you count by 10s?

Write the numbers to complete each equation.

1.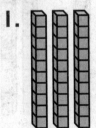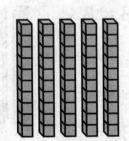

_____ tens + _____ tens = _____ tens

_____ + _____ = _____

2.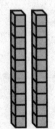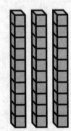

_____ tens + _____ tens = _____ tens

_____ + _____ = _____

**Topic 10** | Lesson 1     Digital Resources at PearsonRealize.com     five hundred forty-seven **547**

Write the numbers to complete each equation.

**3.** © **MP.I Make Sense** Carl and Tina buy some boxes of ice pops. Carl buys 3 boxes. Tina buys 4 boxes. Each box of ice pops is enough for 10 people. For how many people do Carl and Tina have enough ice pops?

_____ + _____ = _____

_____ people

**4.** © **MP.I Make Sense** Rebecca and Brian each have 4 packs of batteries. Each pack has 10 batteries. How many batteries do Rebecca and Brian have in all?

_____ + _____ = _____

_____ batteries

**5.** **Higher Order Thinking** Explain how solving $8 + 2$ can help you solve $80 + 20$.

_____

_____

_____

_____

**6.** © **Assessment** Which equation matches the picture?

Ⓐ $5 + 3 = 8$

Ⓑ $50 + 30 = 80$

Ⓒ $50 + 3 = 53$

Ⓓ $5 + 30 = 35$

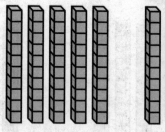

Name _____

**Another Look!** You can mentally add 10 to any number.

$$34 + 10 = \underline{\phantom{44}}$$

Imagine moving down 1 square on a hundred chart.

Or add 1 to the tens digit.

3 + 1 = 4, so 3 tens + 1 ten = 4 tens. The ones digit stays the same.

**HOME ACTIVITY** Choose a number between 1 and 100. Ask your child to add 10 to the number and tell you the sum.

| 21 | 22 | 23 | 24 | 25 | 26 | 27 | 28 | 29 | 30 |
|----|----|----|----|----|----|----|----|----|----|
| 31 | 32 | 33 | 34 | 35 | 36 | 37 | 38 | 39 | 40 |
| 41 | 42 | 43 | 44 | 45 | 46 | 47 | 48 | 49 | 50 |

$$34 + 10 = \underline{44}$$

Use mental math to solve each equation.

1. $55 + 10 = \underline{\phantom{xxx}}$

2. $10 + 10 = \underline{\phantom{xxx}}$

3. $83 + 10 = \underline{\phantom{xxx}}$

4. $16 + 10 = \underline{\phantom{xxx}}$

5. $15 + 10 = \underline{\phantom{xxx}}$

6. $36 + 10 = \underline{\phantom{xxx}}$

Use mental math to solve each problem below.

**7.** $22 + 10 =$ _____

**8.** $47 + 10 =$ _____

**9.** $78 + 10 =$ _____

**10.** $58 + 10 =$ _____

**11.** $14 + 10 =$ _____

**12.** $59 + 10 =$ _____

**13.** $85 + 10 =$ _____

**14.** $52 + 10 =$ _____

**15.** $38 + 10 =$ _____

**16. Higher Order Thinking** Ms. Frank's class has had 63 different spelling words. On Tuesday, they get some more words.

Now the class has had 73 words. How many spelling words did the class get on Tuesday?

_____ words

**17.** © **Assessment** Match each pair of addends with their sum.

| | |
|---|---|
| 75 | $28 + 10$ |
| 64 | $65 + 10$ |
| 38 | $19 + 10$ |
| 47 | $54 + 10$ |
| 29 | $37 + 10$ |

© Pearson Education, Inc. 1

Name _____

**Another Look!** You can use a hundred chart to add 2 two-digit numbers.

24 + 30 = ?

Start at 24.

Move down 3 rows to add 30.

You stop at _54_ .

So, 24 + 30 = _54_ .

| 1 | 2 | 3 | 4 | 5 | 6 | 7 | 8 | 9 | 10 |
|---|---|---|---|---|---|---|---|---|---|
| 11 | 12 | 13 | 14 | 15 | 16 | 17 | 18 | 19 | 20 |
| 21 | 22 | 23 | 24 | 25 | 26 | 27 | 28 | 29 | 30 |
| 31 | 32 | 33 | 34 | 35 | 36 | 37 | 38 | 39 | 40 |
| 41 | 42 | 43 | 44 | 45 | 46 | 47 | 48 | 49 | 50 |
| 51 | 52 | 53 | 54 | 55 | 56 | 57 | 58 | 59 | 60 |
| 61 | 62 | 63 | 64 | 65 | 66 | 67 | 68 | 69 | 70 |
| 71 | 72 | 73 | 74 | 75 | 76 | 77 | 78 | 79 | 80 |
| 81 | 82 | 83 | 84 | 85 | 86 | 87 | 88 | 89 | 90 |
| 91 | 92 | 93 | 94 | 95 | 96 | 97 | 98 | 99 | 100 |

**HOME ACTIVITY** Use a hundred chart. Give your child a one-digit number, such as 7. Have him or her add a multiple of 10, such as 30. Repeat with other one-digit numbers and other two-digit numbers.

 Use a hundred chart to add 2 two-digit numbers.

1.  10
  + 36

2.  15
  + 8

3.  20
  + 58

4.  11
  + 40

5.  40
  + 13

6.  7
  + 34

Topic 10 | Lesson 3   Digital Resources at PearsonRealize.com   five hundred fifty-nine **559**

Count by 10s to find each missing number.

**7. Number Sense** 5, 15, _____, 35, _____

**8. Number Sense** 9, _____, 29, 39, _____

**9. Higher Order Thinking** Mike has 8 marbles. He buys some more. Now he has 28 marbles. How many marbles did Mike buy?

Draw a picture to solve.

Mike bought _____ marbles.

Use the hundred chart to solve each problem.

| 1 | 2 | 3 | 4 | 5 | 6 | 7 | 8 | 9 | 10 |
|---|---|---|---|---|---|---|---|---|---|
| 11 | 12 | 13 | 14 | 15 | 16 | 17 | 18 | 19 | 20 |
| 21 | 22 | 23 | 24 | 25 | 26 | 27 | 28 | 29 | 30 |
| 31 | 32 | 33 | 34 | 35 | 36 | 37 | 38 | 39 | 40 |
| 41 | 42 | 43 | 44 | 45 | 46 | 47 | 48 | 49 | 50 |
| 51 | 52 | 53 | 54 | 55 | 56 | 57 | 58 | 59 | 60 |
| 61 | 62 | 63 | 64 | 65 | 66 | 67 | 68 | 69 | 70 |
| 71 | 72 | 73 | 74 | 75 | 76 | 77 | 78 | 79 | 80 |
| 81 | 82 | 83 | 84 | 85 | 86 | 87 | 88 | 89 | 90 |
| 91 | 92 | 93 | 94 | 95 | 96 | 97 | 98 | 99 | 100 |

**10. © Assessment** Which equation is **NOT** true? Choose all that apply.

☐ $1 + 10 = 11$      ☐ $8 + 60 = 78$

☐ $3 + 70 = 73$      ☐ $8 + 40 = 84$

**11. © Assessment** Which do **NOT** show the missing number? Choose all that apply.

$6 +$ ___?___ $= 76$

☐ 70      ☐ 10

☐ 60      ☐ 7

© Pearson Education, Inc. 1

Name _____

Homework
& Practice  10-4

Add Tens and
Ones Using
an Open
Number Line

**Another Look!** Solve addition problems on number lines using different strategies. Show $30 + 29$ on a number line.

Start with 30. Add tens.
Then add ones.

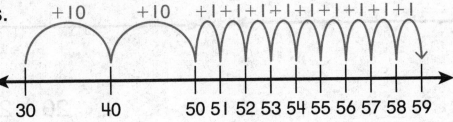

Start with 29. Add tens.

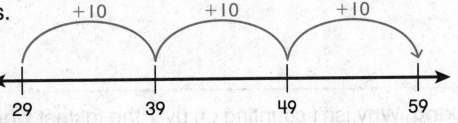

**HOME ACTIVITY** Draw a blank number line on a piece of paper. Give your child an addition equation involving a two-digit number and a one-digit number and ask him or her to add the equation using the number line.

It's better to start with the number that makes it easier to add on the number line.

$30 + 29 = \underline{59}$

Add using the number lines.

1. ⟵――――――――――――――――――――――⟶

$80 + 18 = \underline{\quad}$

2. ⟵――――――――――――――――――――――⟶

$60 + 24 = \underline{\quad}$

**3.** Count on by 1s to solve $42 + 7$.

$$42 + 7 = \rule{2cm}{0.4pt}$$

**4.** Count on by 5s to solve $20 + 25$.

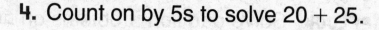

$$20 + 25 = \rule{2cm}{0.4pt}$$

**5. Higher Order Thinking** Why isn't counting on by 1 the fastest way to add $20 + 26$ on a number line?

_____

_____

**6. ⊚ Assessment** Solve $42 + 30$ on an open number line. Show your work.

$$42 + 30 = \rule{2cm}{0.4pt}$$

Name _____

Help    Tools    Games

**Another Look!** Drawing tens and ones can help you add.

*The lines are tens and the dots are ones!*

$50 + 8 = $ _58_

$23 + 6 = $ _29_

**HOME ACTIVITY** Give your child a multiple of 10, such as 50. Have him or her add a one-digit number such as 4. Repeat with other multiples of 10 and one-digit numbers.

Add. Draw blocks to show your work.

**I.**

$20 + 2 = $ _____

**2.**

$45 + 30 = $ _____

**Topic 10** | Lesson 5     Digital Resources at PearsonRealize.com     five hundred seventy-one **571**

Write an equation to model each story problem. Draw blocks to help if needed.

**3.** Andy has 19 markers. He gets 21 more markers. How many markers does Andy have now?

_____ = _____ + _____

_____ markers

**4. Math and Science** Ted counts 30 stars one night. Another night, he counts 5 stars. How many stars did Ted see in all on both nights?

_____ = _____ + _____

_____ stars

Write the missing number for each problem.

**5. Algebra**

$70 + \underline{\qquad} = 76$

**6. Algebra**

$\underline{\qquad} + 8 = 28$

**7. Algebra**

$50 + 3 = \underline{\qquad}$

**8. Higher Order Thinking** Jon has 4 pencils. He gets more from friends. Now he has 24 pencils. How many pencils did Jon get from friends? Draw a picture to solve.

_____ pencils

**9. © Assessment** Find the missing number.

$71 + \underline{\ ?\ } = 77$

Ⓐ 6
Ⓑ 10
Ⓒ 60
Ⓓ 70

© Pearson Education, Inc. 1

Name _____

**Another Look!** You can draw place-value blocks to find 24 + 8.

Can you make a 10?

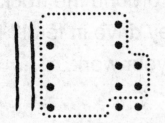

Yes, I can make a 10!

**HOME ACTIVITY** Ask your child to use pennies to find the sum of 26 + 5. Have your child make groups of 10 to explain the answer.

There are ___3___ tens and ___2___ ones.

24 + 8 = ___32___

Draw blocks to add. Do you need to make a 10? Circle **Yes** or **No**.

1.

28 + 3 = _____

Make a 10?

Yes    No

2.

47 + 7 = _____

Make a 10?

Yes    No

3.

55 + 6 = _____

Make a 10?

Yes    No

Solve each problem below.

4. © **MP.5 Use Tools** Susy has 16 pennies saved. She finds 6 more pennies. How many pennies does Susy have now? Draw blocks to show your work.

_____ + _____ = _____   _____ pennies

5. © **MP.5 Use Tools** Hank drives 26 laps around the go-kart track. Allie drives 7 laps around the track. How many laps did they drive in total? Draw blocks to show your work.

_____ + _____ = _____   _____ laps

6. **Higher Order Thinking** Jean adds 35 and 9. How can she solve using only equations to model her thinking? Explain.

_____

_____

_____

_____

7. © **Assessment** Sally adds 9 to 27. Explain how she can use the make 10 strategy to solve the problem.

_____

_____

_____

_____

© Pearson Education, Inc. 1

Name _____

**Another Look!** Sometimes you need to make a 10 when you add.

8 ones + 7 ones = 15 ones.
You can make a 10 with the 15 ones.

When there are more than 9 ones, you need to make a 10.

You add and have 5 tens and 5 ones.

| Tens | Ones |
|------|------|
| 2 | 8 |
| + 2 | 7 |

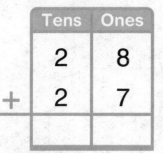

| Tens | Ones |
|------|------|
| 2 | 8 |
| + 2 | 7 |
| 5 | 5 |

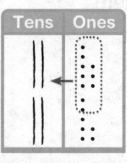

**HOME ACTIVITY** In this activity, use dimes for 10s and pennies for 1s. Ask your child to use dimes and pennies (or two different objects) to find 18 + 27. When your child sees that he or she has 15 pennies, encourage him or her to make a 10 by trading 10 of the pennies for a dime. Repeat with other two-digit + two-digit addition problems.

Draw blocks to add. Do you need to make a 10? Circle **Yes** or **No**.

1.

| Tens | Ones |
|------|------|
| 4 | 2 |
| + 1 | 7 |
| | |

| Tens | Ones |
|------|------|
| | |
| | |

Make a 10?     Yes     No

2.

| Tens | Ones |
|------|------|
| 3 | 3 |
| + 2 | 8 |
| | |

| Tens | Ones |
|------|------|
| | |
| | |

Make a 10?     Yes     No

3. © **MP.2 Reasoning** Seth collects model sailboats. He has 34 large boats. He has 26 small boats. How many model sailboats does Seth have in all? Write an equation to show the problem.

\_\_\_\_\_ + \_\_\_\_\_ = \_\_\_\_\_ \_\_\_\_\_ sailboats

4. © **MP.2 Reasoning** Maria claps 15 times. Then she claps 22 more times. How many times does she clap in all? Write an equation to show the problem.

\_\_\_\_\_ + \_\_\_\_\_ = \_\_\_\_\_ \_\_\_\_\_ claps

5. **Higher Order Thinking** Write two addends that you will **NOT** need to make a 10 to add. Then solve.

| Tens | Ones |
|------|------|
|      |      |
| +    |      |
|      |      |

6. © **Assessment** For which addition equations can you make a 10 to add? Choose all that apply.

☐ $24 + 14 =$ \_\_?\_\_

☐ $17 + 25 =$ \_\_?\_\_

☐ $16 + 13 =$ \_\_?\_\_

☐ $26 + 14 =$ \_\_?\_\_

© Pearson Education, Inc. 1

Name _____

**Another Look!** You draw blocks to find 34 + 18.

Can you make a 10?

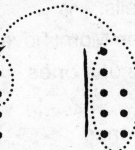

There are ___5___ tens.

There are ___2___ ones.

34 + 18 = __52__

 Yes, I can make a 10!

HOME ACTIVITY Make place-value blocks out of paper (long strips for tens-rods and squares for ones cubes) or use objects to represent grouped tens and separate ones. Write a two-digit + two-digit equation, such as 35 + 17. Ask your child to model the problem, then make a 10 to solve. Repeat with similar problems.

 Find each sum. Solve any way you choose. Draw or explain what you did.

1.

49 + 14 = _____

2.

56 + 10 = _____

Find each sum. Solve any way you choose.

3. **© MP.2 Reasoning** Selena has 27 silver coins. She has 30 copper coins. How many coins does Selena have in all?

_____ coins

4. **ⒶⓏ Vocabulary** Marni collects shells. She has 33 gray shells. She has 37 white shells. How many shells does Marni have? Write how many **tens** and **ones**.

_____ tens _____ ones _____ shells

5. **Higher Order Thinking** Edgar collects sports T-shirts. He has 16 soccer T-shirts and 24 rugby T-shirts. He has 12 hats. How many T-shirts does Edgar have in all? Draw a picture and write an equation to show your work.

_____ T-shirts

6. **© Assessment** Oscar uses place-value blocks to show 87 + 9. Which of the following model this problem? Choose all that apply.

☐    ☐    ☐

© Pearson Education, Inc. 1

**Show the Word**

Color these sums and differences. Leave the rest white.

| 8 | 6 | 9 |

**I can ...**
add and subtract within 10.

© Content Standard 1.OA.C.6

| | | | | | | | | |
|---|---|---|---|---|---|---|---|---|
| $4 + 2$ | $9 - 3$ | $0 + 6$ | $10 - 2$ | $3 + 1$ | $5 + 3$ | $5 + 4$ | $10 - 1$ | $9 + 0$ |
| $6 - 0$ | $8 - 7$ | $8 - 2$ | $4 + 4$ | $1 + 2$ | $8 - 0$ | $6 + 1$ | $8 + 1$ | $5 - 5$ |
| $3 + 3$ | $6 + 0$ | $7 - 1$ | $3 + 5$ | $5 - 3$ | $2 + 6$ | $0 + 2$ | $9 - 0$ | $2 + 8$ |
| $2 + 4$ | $4 + 3$ | $3 + 2$ | $8 + 0$ | $4 - 4$ | $7 + 1$ | $2 - 1$ | $4 + 5$ | $1 + 1$ |
| $10 - 4$ | $2 + 2$ | $6 - 6$ | $6 + 2$ | $9 - 1$ | $0 + 8$ | $4 + 0$ | $0 + 9$ | $8 - 3$ |

**The word is**

_____  _____  _____

Glossary

## Understand Vocabulary

1. Use the models to add the tens.

_____ tens + _____ tens = _____ tens

2. Use the models to add the tens.

_____ tens + _____ tens = _____ tens

3. Add the tens and ones. Do you need to make a 10?

Circle **Yes** or **No**.

25 + 6

Yes           No

4. Add the tens and ones. Do you need to make a 10?

Circle **Yes** or **No**.

74 + 5

Yes           No

5. Add the tens and ones. Do you need to make a 10?

Circle **Yes** or **No**.

52 + 4

Yes           No

## Use Vocabulary in Writing

6. Solve 20 + 6 using an open number line.

   Explain how you solved it using terms from the Word List.

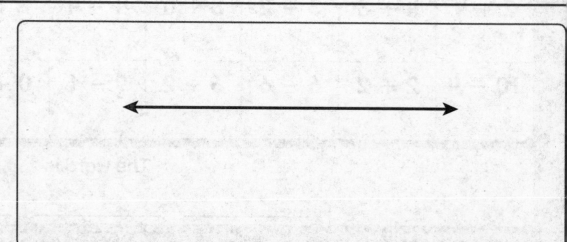

Name _____

**Set A**

You can add groups of 10.

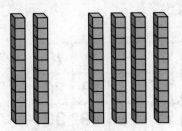

___2___ tens + ___4___ tens = ___6___ tens

__20__ + __40__ = __60__

Write the numbers to complete each equation.

1.

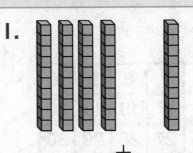

_____ + _____ = _____

2.

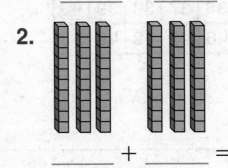

_____ + _____ = _____

**Set B**

You can also use mental math to add ten. When you add 10, the tens digit goes up by 1. The ones digit stays the same.

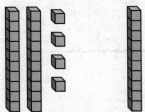

2 tens + 1 ten = 3 tens

24 + 10 = __34__

Count the tens and ones. Then write the number.

3. 36 + 10 = _____

4. 53 + 10 = _____

5. 71 + 10 = _____

You can use part of a hundred chart to add tens and ones.

$$3 + 40 = ?$$

| 1 | 2 | 3 | 4 | 5 | 6 | 7 | 8 | 9 | 10 |
|---|---|---|---|---|---|---|---|---|----|
| 11 | 12 | 13 | 14 | 15 | 16 | 17 | 18 | 19 | 20 |
| 21 | 22 | 23 | 24 | 25 | 26 | 27 | 28 | 29 | 30 |
| 31 | 32 | 33 | 34 | 35 | 36 | 37 | 38 | 39 | 40 |
| 41 | 42 | 43 | 44 | 45 | 46 | 47 | 48 | 49 | 50 |

$$3 + 40 = \underline{43}$$

Use the part of the hundred chart to add tens and ones.

| 1 | 2 | 3 | 4 | 5 | 6 | 7 | 8 | 9 | 10 |
|---|---|---|---|---|---|---|---|---|----|
| 11 | 12 | 13 | 14 | 15 | 16 | 17 | 18 | 19 | 20 |
| 21 | 22 | 23 | 24 | 25 | 26 | 27 | 28 | 29 | 30 |
| 31 | 32 | 33 | 34 | 35 | 36 | 37 | 38 | 39 | 40 |
| 41 | 42 | 43 | 44 | 45 | 46 | 47 | 48 | 49 | 50 |
| 51 | 52 | 53 | 54 | 55 | 56 | 57 | 58 | 59 | 60 |

6. $4 + 50 = $ _____    7. $8 + 30 = $ _____

You can use an open number line to add.

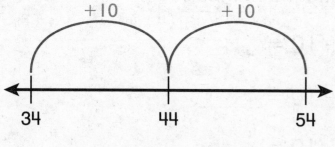

$$34 + 20 = \underline{54}$$

Use an open number line to add.

8.

$$11 + 6 = $$ _____

© Pearson Education, Inc. 1

Name _____

**Set E**

You can use blocks to add tens to a number.

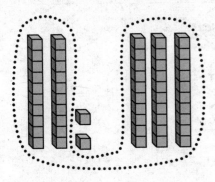

$22 + 30 = \underline{52}$

Add the tens and the ones. Use blocks to help you.

9. $44 + 30 = \underline{\hphantom{000}}$

10. $20 + 5 = \underline{\hphantom{000}}$

11. $30 + 28 = \underline{\hphantom{000}}$

12. $19 + 60 = \underline{\hphantom{000}}$

**Set F**

Sometimes you can make 10 when you add.

$27 + 6 = ?$

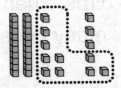

$27 + 3 + 3$

$30 + 3 = \underline{33}$

So, $27 + 6 = \underline{33}$.

Use place-value blocks to solve each problem. Can you make 10?

| | Show | Add | Can you make a 10? | | Find the sum |
|---|---|---|---|---|---|
| 13. | 33 | 9 | Yes | No | |
| 14. | 21 | 7 | Yes | No | |

When you add using place value, you sometimes need to make a 10.

| Tens | Ones |
|------|------|

| Tens | Ones |
|------|------|
| 3 | 4 |
| + 2 | 8 |
| 6 | 2 |

Add. Use blocks. Do you need to make a 10? Circle **Yes** or **No**

15.

| Tens | Ones |
|------|------|
| 2 | 4 |
| + 1 | 9 |
|  |  |

Make a 10?        Yes        No

**Thinking Habits**

Model with Math

Can I use a drawing, diagram, table, or graph to model the problem?

Can I write an equation to show the problem?

Use drawings to show and solve the problem. Then write the equation.

16. Sally sees 15 birds. Then she sees 17 more. How many birds did Sally see in all?

____ + ____ = ____

© Pearson Education, Inc. 1

# Use Models and Strategies to Subtract Tens

**Essential Question:** How can I use what I know about subtraction to subtract tens?

People develop all kinds of tools to solve problems and make our lives easier.

Sometimes they just take a tool that already exists and make it better.

Wow! Let's do this project and learn more.

## Math and Science Project: Tools Solve Problems

**Find Out** Talk to friends and relatives about different tools we use to solve problems. Ask them about tools they use in their everyday lives.

**Journal: Make a Book** Show what you found out. In your book, also:
- Draw some tools that solve simple problems. Make sure to describe the simple problems they solve.
- Make up and solve subtraction problems about tools.

Name _____

# Review What You Know

**A-Z Vocabulary**

**1.** How many **tens** are in this number?

23

_____ tens

**2.** Use the **hundred chart** to count by 10s.

| 1 | 2 | 3 | 4 | 5 | 6 | 7 | 8 | 9 | 10 |
|---|---|---|---|---|---|---|---|---|----|
| 11 | 12 | 13 | 14 | 15 | 16 | 17 | 18 | 19 | 20 |
| 21 | 22 | 23 | 24 | 25 | 26 | 27 | 28 | 29 | 30 |
| 31 | 32 | 33 | 34 | 35 | 36 | 37 | 38 | 39 | 40 |
| 41 | 42 | 43 | 44 | 45 | 46 | 47 | 48 | 49 | 50 |
| 51 | 52 | 53 | 54 | 55 | 56 | 57 | 58 | 59 | 60 |
| 61 | 62 | 63 | 64 | 65 | 66 | 67 | 68 | 69 | 70 |
| 71 | 72 | 73 | 74 | 75 | 76 | 77 | 78 | 79 | 80 |
| 81 | 82 | 83 | 84 | 85 | 86 | 87 | 88 | 89 | 90 |
| 91 | 92 | 93 | 94 | 95 | 96 | 97 | 98 | 99 | 100 |

30, 40, 50, _____, _____

**3.** Use the **open number line** to add.

$\longleftarrow\longrightarrow$

$7 + 9 =$ _____

## Count Back to Subtract

**4.** Mark takes 8 pictures. Julia takes 3 fewer pictures than Mark. Count back to find how many pictures Julia took.

8, _____, _____

_____ pictures

**5.** Katie picks 15 flowers. Max picks 13 flowers. Count back to find how many fewer flowers Max picked than Katie.

15, _____, _____

_____ fewer flowers

## Subtraction Facts

**6.** Find each difference.

$12 - 4 =$ _____

$14 - 7 =$ _____

$19 - 9 =$ _____

© Pearson Education, Inc. 1

Name _____

**Another Look!** If you know how to subtract ones, you can subtract tens.

$$40 - 20 = ?$$

40 − 20 is the same as
4 tens − 2 tens.

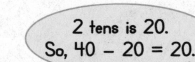
2 tens is 20.
So, 40 − 20 = 20.

4 tens − 2 tens = 2 tens

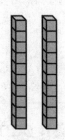

$$40 - 20 = \underline{20}$$

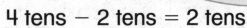

HOME ACTIVITY Use cups and small household objects such as buttons or paperclips. Put out eight cups and put ten items in each cup. Have your child count the items. Then take away one or two of the cups and ask how many items are left. Repeat the activity and ask your child to write an equation to show how many items are left.

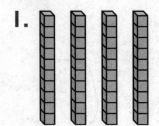
Cross out the blocks as needed to solve.

I. _____ tens − 3 tens = _____ ten

_____ − _____ = _____

2. 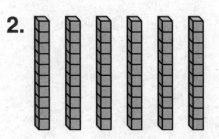 _____ tens − 2 tens = _____ tens

_____ − _____ = _____

Cross out the blocks as needed and solve the problems.

3.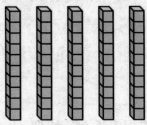

_____ tens − 3 tens = _____ tens

_____ − _____ = _____

4.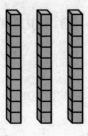

_____ tens − 1 ten = _____ tens

_____ − _____ = _____

5. **Math and Science** Meg makes a tool to crush cans. She has 70 cans. She crushes 20 cans. How many cans does Meg still need to crush? Write an equation. Then solve.

_____ − _____ = _____ cans

6. **Higher Order Thinking** Write and solve a story problem for 80 − 50.

_____

_____

_____

_____

7. © **Assessment** Which shows the answer to 7 tens − 3 tens?

Ⓐ 20

Ⓑ 30

Ⓒ 40

Ⓓ 50

Name _____

**Another Look!** You can use a hundred chart to subtract tens.

**50 − 30 = ?**

30 is ___3___ tens

*For every ten I take away, I move up 1 row on the hundred chart.*

| 1 | 2 | 3 | 4 | 5 | 6 | 7 | 8 | 9 | 10 |
|---|---|---|---|---|---|---|---|---|----|
| 11 | 12 | 13 | 14 | 15 | 16 | 17 | 18 | 19 | 20 |
| 21 | 22 | 23 | 24 | 25 | 26 | 27 | 28 | 29 | 30 |
| 31 | 32 | 33 | 34 | 35 | 36 | 37 | 38 | 39 | 40 |
| 41 | 42 | 43 | 44 | 45 | 46 | 47 | 48 | 49 | (50) |

**50 − 30 = ___20___**

**HOME ACTIVITY** Practice counting forward and backwards by 10s with your child. Try counting only some of the sequence and then having your child pick up where you left off. You can also try alternating numbers with him or her.

Use the partial hundred chart to solve each problem.

| 41 | 42 | 43 | 44 | 45 | 46 | 47 | 48 | 49 | 50 |
|----|----|----|----|----|----|----|----|----|----|
| 51 | 52 | 53 | 54 | 55 | 56 | 57 | 58 | 59 | 60 |
| 61 | 62 | 63 | 64 | 65 | 66 | 67 | 68 | 69 | 70 |
| 71 | 72 | 73 | 74 | 75 | 76 | 77 | 78 | 79 | 80 |

1. 80 − 30 = _____

2. 70 − 10 = _____

3. 80 − 20 = _____

4. 60 − 10 = _____

Use the hundred chart to subtract.

| 1 | 2 | 3 | 4 | 5 | 6 | 7 | 8 | 9 | 10 |
|---|---|---|---|---|---|---|---|---|----|
| 11 | 12 | 13 | 14 | 15 | 16 | 17 | 18 | 19 | 20 |
| 21 | 22 | 23 | 24 | 25 | 26 | 27 | 28 | 29 | 30 |
| 31 | 32 | 33 | 34 | 35 | 36 | 37 | 38 | 39 | 40 |
| 41 | 42 | 43 | 44 | 45 | 46 | 47 | 48 | 49 | 50 |
| 51 | 52 | 53 | 54 | 55 | 56 | 57 | 58 | 59 | 60 |
| 61 | 62 | 63 | 64 | 65 | 66 | 67 | 68 | 69 | 70 |
| 71 | 72 | 73 | 74 | 75 | 76 | 77 | 78 | 79 | 80 |
| 81 | 82 | 83 | 84 | 85 | 86 | 87 | 88 | 89 | 90 |
| 91 | 92 | 93 | 94 | 95 | 96 | 97 | 98 | 99 | 100 |

5. $20 - 10 =$ _____

6. $90 - 30 =$ _____

7. $80 - 30 =$ _____

8. $80 - 40 =$ _____

9. $60 - 40 =$ _____

10. $70 - 20 =$ _____

11. $80 - 80 =$ _____

12. $20 - 10 =$ _____

13. $80 - 50 =$ _____

14. $90 - 20 =$ _____

15. **Higher Order Thinking** How can you use a hundred chart to solve $90 - 80$?

Solve the problem. Then explain how you got your answer.

$$90 - 80 = \underline{\quad}$$

_____

_____

_____

16. © **Assessment** Ms. Rodin has 30 spelling tests to grade in all. She has graded 10 of them already.

How many spelling tests does she have left to grade?

Ⓐ 10

Ⓑ 20

Ⓒ 30

Ⓓ 40

© Pearson Education, Inc. 1

Name _____

**Another Look!** You can use an open number line to subtract.

Find 90 − 50.

Start by marking 90 on the number line.

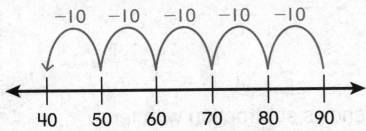

−10   −10   −10   −10   −10

40   50   60   70   80   90

Count back by tens until you have subtracted 50.

What number did you land on? __40__

Since you are counting back, 90 should be on the right side.

**HOME ACTIVITY** Give your child the following subtraction problems to solve: 20 − 10, 90 − 30, 80 − 50, and 30 − 30. First, ask your child to draw an open number line and solve each problem. If he/she struggles, help by drawing the open number line or marking the first number on the number line.

Use number lines to subtract.

1.

←————————————————→

80 − 40 = _____

2.

←————————————————→

70 − _____ = 10

**3.**

$$40 - 30 = \underline{\hspace{2cm}}$$

**4. Higher Order Thinking** Write an equation that shows subtraction with tens. Show the problem on the open number line and solve.

$$\underline{\hspace{1.5cm}} - \underline{\hspace{1.5cm}} = \underline{\hspace{1.5cm}}$$

**5. © Assessment** Solve $90 - 40$ on an open number line. Explain your work.

© Pearson Education, Inc. 1

Name _____

**Solve & Share**

Solve the subtraction problem. Use the strategy you think works best and explain why.

**I can ...**
use addition to subtract tens.

© Content Standard 1.NBT.C.6
Mathematical Practices MP.2, MP.3, MP.4, MP.7

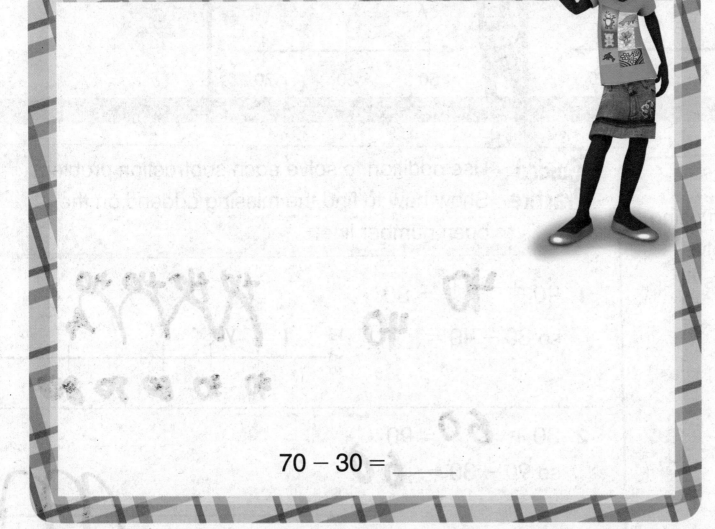

$70 - 30 = $ _____

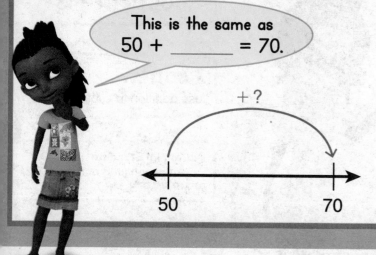

You can use addition to help subtract tens. Find 70 − 50.

This is the same as
50 + _____ = 70.

+?

50    70

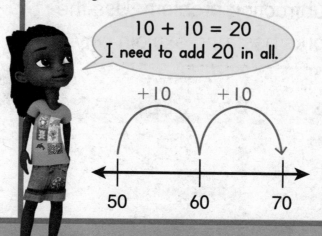

Count by 10s to find the missing number.

10 + 10 = 20
I need to add 20 in all.

+10    +10

50    60    70

Use the missing addend to solve the subtraction problem.

50 + __20__ = 70, so

70 − 50 = __20__.

---

**Do You Understand?**

**Show Me!** How can using addition help you solve subtraction problems?

☆**Guided**☆
**Practice**  Use addition to solve each subtraction problem. Show how to find the missing addend on the open number line.

1. 40 + __40__ = 80,
   so 80 − 40 = __40__.

2. 30 + __60__ = 90,
   so 90 − 30 = __60__.

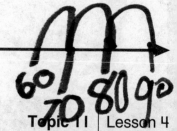

**Independent Practice**  Use addition to solve each subtraction problem. Show how to find the missing addend on the open number line.

3. 20 + **40** = 60, so 60 − 20 = **40**.

4. 30 + **50** = 80, so 80 − 30 = **50**.

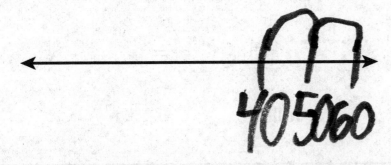

Use addition to solve each subtraction problem. Draw a picture to show your thinking.

5. 30 + _____ = 50, so 50 − 30 = _____.

I can draw tens to show the addend I know and the missing addend.

6. 60 + _____ = 80, so 80 − 60 = _____.

Write an equation and solve the problems below.

7. © **MP.2 Reasoning** Mr. Andrews collects 90 papers from his students. He has already graded 40 papers. How many papers does Mr. Andrews have left to grade?

_____ ◯ _____ = _____

_____ papers

8. © **MP.2 Reasoning** Stacy drives 40 miles to work. She has already driven some miles. Stacy has 20 miles left to drive. How many miles has Stacy already driven?

_____ ◯ _____ = _____

_____ miles

9. **Higher Order Thinking** Sam has 4 cases of juice boxes. There are 10 juice boxes in each case. He brings 3 cases to share with his class.

Write and solve an equation to show how many juice boxes Sam has left.

_____ – _____ = _____

_____ juice boxes

10. © **Assessment** Dr. Tess has 20 patients to see today. She has already seen 10 of them. How many patients does Dr. Tess have left to see?

Ⓐ 40

Ⓑ 30

Ⓒ 20

Ⓓ 10

Name _____

**Another Look!** You can use addition to subtract 10s.

$90 - 50 = ?$     Picture a piece of a hundred chart.

| 41 | 42 | 43 | 44 | 45 | 46 | 47 | 48 | 49 | 50 |
|----|----|----|----|----|----|----|----|----|----|
| 51 | 52 | 53 | 54 | 55 | 56 | 57 | 58 | 59 | 60 |
| 61 | 62 | 63 | 64 | 65 | 66 | 67 | 68 | 69 | 70 |
| 71 | 72 | 73 | 74 | 75 | 76 | 77 | 78 | 79 | 80 |
| 81 | 82 | 83 | 84 | 85 | 86 | 87 | 88 | 89 | 90 |

$50 + \underline{40} = 90$, so

$90 - 50 = \underline{40}$.

If I start on 50, I have to move down 4 to get to 90.

**HOME ACTIVITY** Practice counting by 10s with your child. Start counting at a multiple of 10 and have him or her continue the sequence. Then practice adding different multiples of 10 (10–90 only).

Use addition to solve each subtraction problem. Use the hundred chart above to help, if needed.

1. $50 + \underline{\hspace{1cm}} = 70$, so

$70 - 50 = \underline{\hspace{1cm}}$.

2. $60 + \underline{\hspace{1cm}} = 90$, so

$90 - 60 = \underline{\hspace{1cm}}$.

Use addition to solve each subtraction problem.
Draw a picture to show your thinking.

3. $20 +$ _____ $= 40$, so $40 - 20 =$ _____.

4. $30 +$ _____ $= 80$, so $80 - 30 =$ _____.

5. $60 +$ _____ $= 70$, so $70 - 60 =$ _____.

6. $40 +$ _____ $= 90$, so $90 - 40 =$ _____.

7. **Higher Order Thinking** Jackie plans to paint the fingernails of 8 friends. She finishes painting 4 of her friends' nails. If each friend has ten nails to paint, how many nails does Jackie still need to paint?

Write and solve an equation to show how many more nails Jackie needs to paint.

_____ $-$ _____ $=$ _____

_____ nails

8. © **Assessment** Which addition equation could you use to help you solve the subtraction problem below?

$70 - 20 = ?$

Ⓐ $20 + 10 = 30$

Ⓑ $70 + 20 = 90$

Ⓒ $20 + 50 = 70$

Ⓓ $10 + 10 = 20$

© Pearson Education, Inc. 1

Name _____

**Another Look!** You can mentally subtract 10 from any number.

$72 - 10 = ?$

Imagine moving up 1 row on a hundred chart.

| 51 | 52 | 53 | 54 | 55 | 56 | 57 | 58 | 59 | 60 |
|----|----|----|----|----|----|----|----|----|----|
| 61 | 62 | 63 | 64 | 65 | 66 | 67 | 68 | 69 | 70 |
| 71 | 72 | 73 | 74 | 75 | 76 | 77 | 78 | 79 | 80 |

Or, subtract 1 from the tens digit.

7 tens − 1 ten = 6 tens

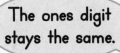
The ones digit stays the same.

$72 - 10 = \underline{62}$

**HOME ACTIVITY** Give your child a 2-digit number and ask him or her to mentally subtract 10 from it. Have your child explain how he or she found the answer. Repeat with other 2-digit numbers.

Use mental math to solve.

1. $85 - 10 = $ _____

2. $37 - 10 = $ _____

3. $59 - 10 = $ _____

4. $41 - 10 = $ _____

5. $75 - 10 = $ _____

6. $16 - 10 = $ _____

Use mental math to solve.

**7.** $29 - 10 = $ _____

**8.** $14 - 10 = $ _____

**9.** $28 - 10 = $ _____

**10.** $45 - 10 = $ _____

**11.** $78 - 10 = $ _____

**12.** $13 - 10 = $ _____

**13. Algebra** Write the missing number in each equation.

$\boxed{\phantom{00}} + 10 = 50$         $50 - \boxed{\phantom{00}} = 40$         $70 - 10 = \boxed{\phantom{00}}$

**14. Higher Order Thinking** Choose two numbers from the list below and write them on the correct lines to make the equation true.

$$25 \quad 34 \quad 45 \quad 55 \quad 68 \quad 72$$

_____ $- 10 = $ _____

**15. ⓒ Assessment** Jon has 77 buttons. He uses 10 of them to make a picture frame. How many buttons does Jon have left? Write and solve the equation for this story.

_____ $-$ _____ $= $ _____

_____ buttons

© Pearson Education, Inc. 1

Name _____

## Solve & Share

Solve the subtraction problem. Use the strategy you think works best. Explain why.

60 − 40 = _____

Josh needs to shovel snow from 50 driveways. He has already shoveled 30 of them. How many driveways does Josh have left to shovel?

**I know 3 different ways to solve this subtraction problem.**

One way to solve the problem is to use a hundred chart.

| 11 | 12 | 13 | 14 | 15 | 16 | 17 | 18 | 19 | 20 |
|----|----|----|----|----|----|----|----|----|----|
| 21 | 22 | 23 | 24 | 25 | 26 | 27 | 28 | 29 | 30 |
| 31 | 32 | 33 | 34 | 35 | 36 | 37 | 38 | 39 | 40 |
| 41 | 42 | 43 | 44 | 45 | 46 | 47 | 48 | 49 | 50 |

$50 - 30 = \underline{20}$

Another way is to use a number line.

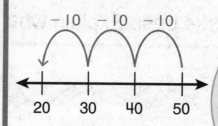

$50 - 30 = \underline{20}$

You can also think addition to subtract.

**He has 30 done already. He has some more to do to get to 50.**
$30 + \underline{20} = 50$, so
$50 - 30 = \underline{20}$.

## Do You Understand?

**Show Me!** Which strategy would you use to solve $50 - 40$? Explain why.

 **Guided Practice** Use the partial hundred chart or another strategy to solve each subtraction problem.

| 31 | 32 | 33 | 34 | 35 | 36 | 37 | 38 | 39 | 40 |
|----|----|----|----|----|----|----|----|----|----|
| 41 | 42 | 43 | 44 | 45 | 46 | 47 | 48 | 49 | 50 |
| 51 | 52 | 53 | 54 | 55 | 56 | 57 | 58 | 59 | 60 |
| 61 | 62 | 63 | 64 | 65 | 66 | 67 | 68 | 69 | 70 |

1. $70 - 10 = \underline{60}$

2. $60 - 20 = \underline{\phantom{00}}$

3. $43 - 10 = \underline{\phantom{00}}$

4. $70 - 30 = \underline{\phantom{00}}$

© Pearson Education, Inc. 1

**Topic 11** | Lesson 6

Tools   Assessment

**Independent Practice**   Use the strategy you think works best to solve each subtraction problem. Explain your reasoning.

**5.** $90 - 20 =$ _____

**6.** $40 - 20 =$ _____

**7.** $80 - 60 =$ _____

**8.** $30 - 20 =$ _____

**9.** $74 - 10 =$ _____

**10.** $80 - 40 =$ _____

**11. Math and Science** Jacob designs a robot that completes an obstacle course in 54 seconds. Clara designs a robot that completes the same course in 10 fewer seconds than Jacob's robot. How many seconds does Clara's robot take to complete the obstacle course? Write an equation to show your work.

_____ $-$ _____ $=$ _____          _____ seconds

Choose one of the strategies you learned to solve each subtraction problem.

**12. © MP.5 Use Tools** Charlie puts baseball cards into an album. He already put 10 cards in the album. He has 83 cards in all.

How many baseball cards does Charlie have left to put in the album?

_____ cards

**13. © MP.5 Use Tools** Pearl's basketball team scores 50 points in one game. They score some points in the first half. They score 20 points in the second half.

How many points did Pearl's team score in the first half?

_____ points

**14. Higher Order Thinking** Write a subtraction problem for which you would think addition to subtract. Explain why this would be a good strategy to use to solve this problem.

_____

_____

_____

_____

**15. © Assessment** Explain how you would use a hundred chart to solve 60 – 20.

_____

_____

_____

_____

Name _____

**Another Look!** You can use addition to solve subtraction problems.

$80 - 50 = ?$

Change the subtraction equation to an addition equation.

$50 + ? = 80$

Count up from 50 to find the missing number.

50, _60_ , _70_ , _80_

$50 + \underline{30} = 80$, so $80 - 50 = \underline{30}$.

To get to 80, I need to add 10 three times. That is the same as adding 30.

**HOME ACTIVITY** Review subtraction facts to 10 with your child. Talk to him or her about how these facts are related to subtracting tens from numbers to 100. Explain that you are simply subtracting a number of tens rather than a number of ones.

Use the number line to solve the subtraction problems.

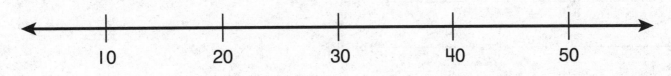

10      20      30      40      50

**1.** $40 - 20 =$ _____

**2.** $50 - 10 =$ _____

**3.** $30 - 20 =$ _____

Solve each problem below.

4. © **MP.3 Explain** Solve $80 - 30$ using any strategy you choose. Tell how you solved the problem.

_____

_____

5. **Number Sense** Write a related addition equation for the subtraction equation below.

$$57 - 10 = 47$$

_____ + _____ = _____

6. **Higher Order Thinking** Would you choose to use a hundred chart to solve $90 - 80$? Why or why not? If not, which strategy would work better?

_____

_____

_____

7. © **Assessment** Explain how you could use a number line to solve $70 - 50$.

_____

_____

_____

_____

_____

© Pearson Education, Inc. 1

Name _____

Solve & Share

Val picks 40 strawberries. She shares 20 of them with her brother. How many strawberries did Val keep for herself?

How can modeling your thinking help you solve this problem?

**I can ...**
model my thinking to solve problems.

© **Mathematical Practices**
MP.4 Also MP.1, MP.5
**Content Standards** 1.NBT.C.5, 1.NBT.C.6

**Thinking Habits**

Can I use a drawing, diagram, graph, or table to model this problem?

How can I make my model better if it doesn't work?

_____ ◯ _____ = _____

Nate has 70 green apples. He has 30 red apples. How many more green apples does Nate have than red ones?

**How can I model this problem?**

I can use pictures, objects, and equations to show and solve this problem. Then I can decide if my model makes sense.

I will draw a picture and write an equation.

$70 - 30 = \underline{40}$

$7 \text{ tens} - 3 \text{ tens} = 4 \text{ tens}$

Nate has __40__ more green apples.

I can show my work in another way!

---

**Do You Understand?**

**Show Me!** In the example above, how do the boxes of 10 help model the problem?

**☆ Guided Practice ☆** Use drawings, models, or equations to solve.

1. A store has 60 muffins. It sells 30 of the muffins. How many muffins does the store have now?

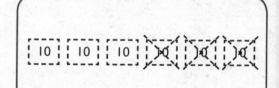

____30____ muffins

---

2. Andy has 84 baseball cards. He gives away 10 cards. How many cards does Andy have now?

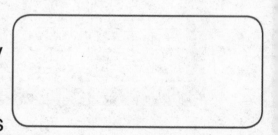

_____ cards

**Topic 11 | Lesson 7**

## Independent Practice ✩ Use drawings, models, or equations to solve. Explain your work.

3. Viola has 80 stickers.
   Dean has 60 stickers.
   How many more stickers
   does Viola have than Dean?

   _____ more stickers

4. Carla has a book with
   50 pages. She reads
   20 pages. How many pages
   does she have left to read?

   _____ pages

5. A store has 72 toy cars.
   It sells 10 cars.
   How many cars does the
   store have left?

   _____ cars

# Math Practices and Problem Solving

**Dog Walking** James, Emily, and Simon walk dogs after school.

On Monday, they have 40 dogs to walk. James and Emily take 20 of the dogs for a walk. How many dogs are left to walk?

6. **MP.1 Make Sense** What problem do you need to solve?

_____

_____

_____

7. **MP.5 Use Tools** What tool or tools can you use to solve this problem?

_____

_____

_____

8. **MP.4 Model** Write an equation to show the problem. Then, use pictures, words, or symbols to solve.

_____ dogs

_____ ◯ _____ = _____

© Pearson Education, Inc. 1

Name _____

**Another Look!** You can use the math you know to solve new problems.

Greg has 30 stickers. He puts 20 stickers into his sticker book.
How many stickers does he have left to put away?

Draw a picture:          Write an equation:

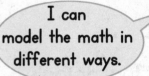
I can model the math in different ways.

$$30 - 20 = ?$$

$$30 - 20 = \underline{10}$$

**HOME ACTIVITY** Give your child a subtraction problem, such as: 70 − 20. Ask her or him to tell you two different strategies for solving this subtraction problem.

---

Use drawings, models, or equations to solve. Show your work.

1. Jon puts 40 songs onto a playlist. He takes 10 songs off. How many songs are still on the playlist?

2. Tammy sees 24 ants. 10 ants go into an anthill. How many ants are left?

## Performance Assessment

**Sock Sorting** Jack puts 80 socks in a basket. He sorts 50 socks into one pile.

How many socks does he still need to sort?

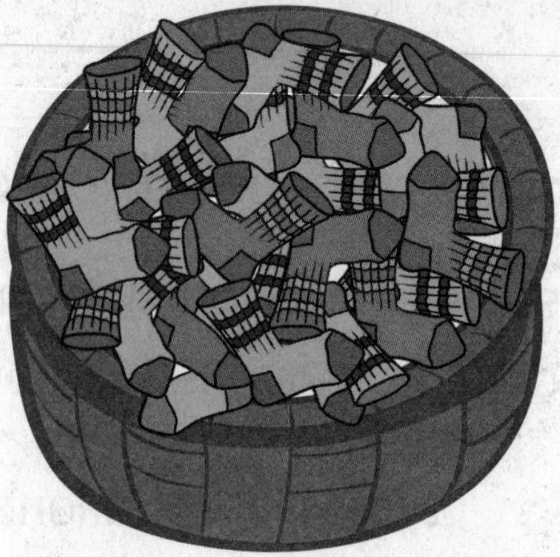

3. **MP.5 Use Tools** What tool or tools would you choose to use to solve this problem?

____________________

____________________

____________________

4. **MP.4 Model** Draw a picture and write an equation to solve this problem.

____ ○ ____ = ____

5. **MP.1 Make Sense** How can you check that your answer makes sense?

____________________

____________________

Name _____

**Point & Tally**

Find a partner. Get paper and a pencil.

Each partner chooses a different color: light blue or dark blue.

Partner 1 and Partner 2 each point to a black number at the same time. Subtract Partner 2's number from Partner 1's number.

If the answer is on your color, you get a tally mark.

Work until one partner gets twelve tally marks.

**I can ...**
add and subtract within 10.

© Content Standard 1.OA.C.6

**Partner 1**

| 10 |
| 5 |
| 7 |
| 8 |
| 9 |
| 6 |

| 3 | 6 | 10 | 9 | 1 | 8 |
| 1 | 7 | 2 | 4 | 0 | 5 |

**Partner 2**

| 0 |
| 3 |
| 5 |
| 1 |
| 4 |
| 2 |

**Tally Marks for Partner 1**

**Tally Marks for Partner 2**

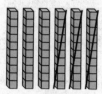
# Vocabulary Review

### Word List
- add
- difference
- number chart
- open number line
- subtract
- tens

## Understand Vocabulary

**1.** Subtract the tens shown by the model.

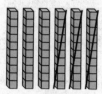

_____ tens — _____ tens

= _____ tens

**2.** Subtract the tens shown by the model.

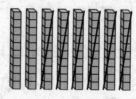

_____ tens — _____ tens

= _____ tens

**3.** Circle the addition problem that could help you solve 50 − 30.

$10 + 40 = 50$

$25 + 25 = 50$

$30 + 20 = 50$

$40 + 10 = 50$

**4.** Solve 40 − 20 using a number chart. Circle the difference.

| 1 | 2 | 3 | 4 | 5 | 6 | 7 | 8 | 9 | 10 |
|---|---|---|---|---|---|---|---|---|----|
| 11 | 12 | 13 | 14 | 15 | 16 | 17 | 18 | 19 | 20 |
| 21 | 22 | 23 | 24 | 25 | 26 | 27 | 28 | 29 | 30 |
| 31 | 32 | 33 | 34 | 35 | 36 | 37 | 38 | 39 | 40 |
| 41 | 42 | 43 | 44 | 45 | 46 | 47 | 48 | 49 | 50 |

**5.** Use mental math to solve 70 − 10. Circle the difference.

40       50

60       70

## Use Vocabulary in Writing

**6.** Solve 80 − 50 using an open number line. Explain how you solved it using terms from the Word List.

Name _____

## Set A

You can subtract tens.

$$40 - 30 = \underline{\quad ? \quad}$$

You need to subtract 30, which is 3 tens.

Cross out that many tens.

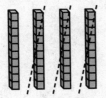

Count the tens and ones that are left.

$$40 - 30 = 10$$

Cross out the tens. Write the difference.

1.
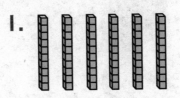

$$60 - 40 = \underline{\quad\quad}$$

2.
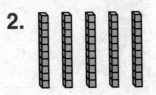

$$50 - 20 = \underline{\quad\quad}$$

## Set B

You can use a hundred chart to subtract tens.

$$80 - 20 = \underline{\quad ? \quad}$$

| 51 | 52 | 53 | 54 | 55 | 56 | 57 | 58 | 59 | 60 |
|----|----|----|----|----|----|----|----|----|----|
| 61 | 62 | 63 | 64 | 65 | 66 | 67 | 68 | 69 | 70 |
| 71 | 72 | 73 | 74 | 75 | 76 | 77 | 78 | 79 | 80 |

$$80 - 20 = 60$$

Use this partial hundred chart to subtract tens.

| 41 | 42 | 43 | 44 | 45 | 46 | 47 | 48 | 49 | 50 |
|----|----|----|----|----|----|----|----|----|----|
| 51 | 52 | 53 | 54 | 55 | 56 | 57 | 58 | 59 | 60 |
| 61 | 62 | 63 | 64 | 65 | 66 | 67 | 68 | 69 | 70 |

3. $70 - 20 = \underline{\quad\quad}$

4. $60 - 10 = \underline{\quad\quad}$

You can use mental math to subtract tens. Find 46 − 10.

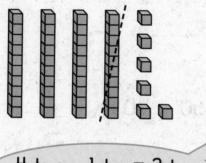

4 tens − 1 ten = 3 tens.
So, 46 − 10 = 36.

Subtract. Use mental math.

5. 62 − 10 = _____

6. 89 − 10 = _____

7. 27 − 10 = _____

**Set D**

## Thinking Habits

**Model with Math**

Can I use a drawing, diagram, table, or graph to model the problem?

How can I make my model better if it doesn't work?

Write an equation to solve. Use drawings or models to show your work.

8. A store has 50 toy boats. They sell 10 boats. How many toy boats does the store have now?

_____ toy boats

Name _____

## Fred's Farm

Fred sells different vegetables at his farm. He puts them in packages of 10.

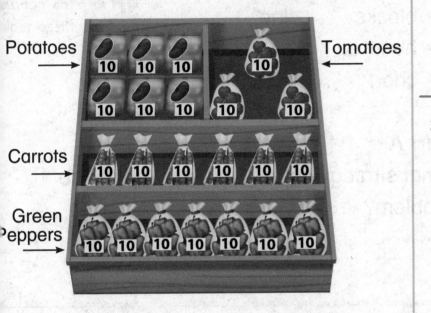

Potatoes → 

Tomatoes ←

Carrots →

Green Peppers →

**1.** Fred sells 3 packages of green peppers. How many green peppers does he have left to sell?
Use the open number line to solve.

←————————————————→

_____ green peppers

**2.** Fred feeds 10 carrots to his horse. How many carrots does he have left?

_____ carrots

**3.** Fred sells 30 potatoes on Monday. He sells the rest on Tuesday. How many potatoes were sold on Tuesday?
Use the partial hundred chart to solve the problem. Write the missing numbers in the equation.

| 21 | 22 | 23 | 24 | 25 | 26 | 27 | 28 | 29 | 30 |
|----|----|----|----|----|----|----|----|----|----|
| 31 | 32 | 33 | 34 | 35 | 36 | 37 | 38 | 39 | 40 |
| 41 | 42 | 43 | 44 | 45 | 46 | 47 | 48 | 49 | 50 |
| 51 | 52 | 53 | 54 | 55 | 56 | 57 | 58 | 59 | 60 |
| 61 | 62 | 63 | 64 | 65 | 66 | 67 | 68 | 69 | 70 |
| 71 | 72 | 73 | 74 | 75 | 76 | 77 | 78 | 79 | 80 |

_____ ◯ _____ = _____

_____ potatoes

**4.** Debbie buys 4 packages of carrots at the farm. She uses 10 carrots to make soup. How many carrots does she have left?

Solve the problem. Use one of the strategies you learned. Show how you solved the problem.

- number line
- hundred chart
- think addition to subtract
- blocks

_____ carrots

**5.** Ty buys 36 vegetables. Lee buys 10 fewer vegetables than Ty. How many vegetables does Lee buy?

- picture
- blocks
- hundred chart
- number line
- another tool

You can use these tools

### Part A
What strategy could you use to solve the problem?

_____

_____

### Part B
Write an equation and solve the problem. Show how you solved it.

____ ◯ ____ = ____

_____ vegetables

# TOPIC 12 Measure Lengths

**Essential Question:** What are ways to measure how long an object is?

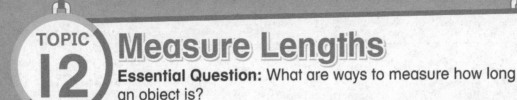

*People cannot see in the dark.*

*Some animals can make themselves light up or glow in the dark.*

*Wow! Let's do this project and learn more.*

## Math and Science Project: Now You See Me, Now You Don't!

**Find Out** Talk to friends and relatives about animals that can be seen in the dark. Ask how some animals can make themselves glow in the dark.

**Journal: Make a Book** Show what you found out. In your book, also:
• Draw pictures of animals that can glow in the dark.
• Think about how you could measure these animals.

Name _____

# Review What You Know

**A-Z Vocabulary**

1. Circle the number that is **less than** the number of cubes.

3  5  8

2. Circle the number that is **greater than** the number of cubes.

1  3  5

3. Circle the symbol that is used to **compare** two numbers

+   –   >

## Comparing Numbers

4. Choose two numbers to make the sentence true.




____ is less than ____.

5. Charlie has 9 stickers. Pearl has 5 stickers. Write the numbers and the symbol to compare their numbers of stickers.



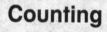

## Counting

6. Write the missing numbers.

6, 7, 8, ____, ____, 11,

____

662   six hundred sixty-two          © Pearson Education, Inc. 1                    **Topic 12**

# My Word Cards

Study the words on the front of the card.
Complete the activity on the back.

A-Z
Glossary

## longest

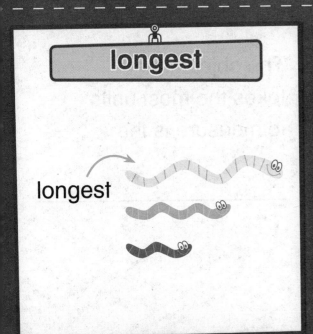

longest

## shortest

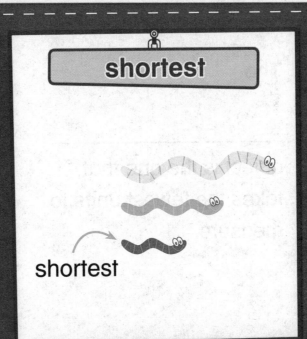

shortest

## longer

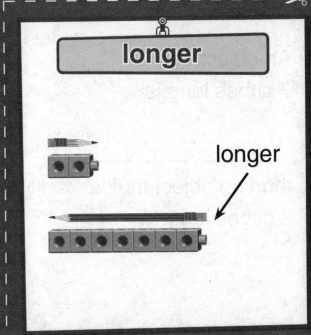

longer

## shorter

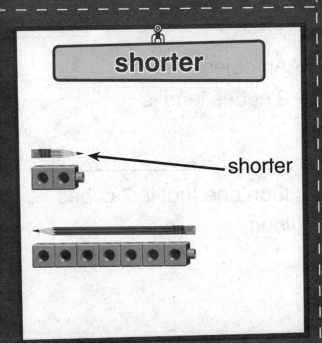

shorter

## length

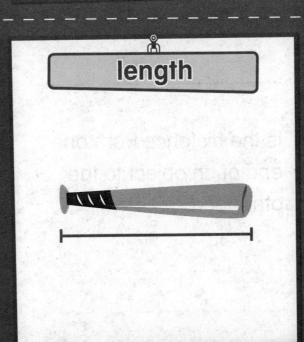

## measure

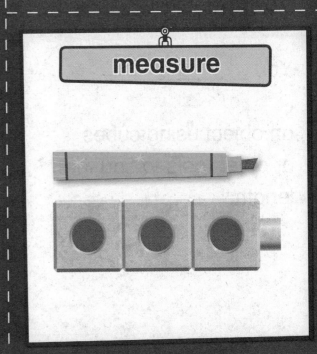

# My Word Cards

Use what you know to complete the sentences.
Extend learning by writing your own sentence using each word.

An object that is 7 cubes long is

____________________

than an object that is 2 cubes long.

The

____________________

object is the one that takes the fewest units to measure.

The object that takes the most units to measure is the

____________________.

You ____________________

an object using cubes or other tools to find the length.

____________________

is the distance from one end of an object to the other end.

An object that is 2 cubes long is

____________________

than one that is 7 cubes long.

# My Word Cards

Study the words on the front of the card.
Complete the activity on the back.

A-Z Glossary

length unit

Use what you know to complete the sentence.
Extend learning by writing your own sentence using each word.

A _____

_____

is the shorter object that you use to measure a longer object.

© Pearson Education, Inc. 1

Name ______________________________

Help Tools Games

# Homework & Practice 12-1

## Compare and Order by Length

**Another Look!** You can find the lengths of objects by comparing them.

Which color of ribbon is the longest? Purple

Which color of ribbon is the shortest? Blue

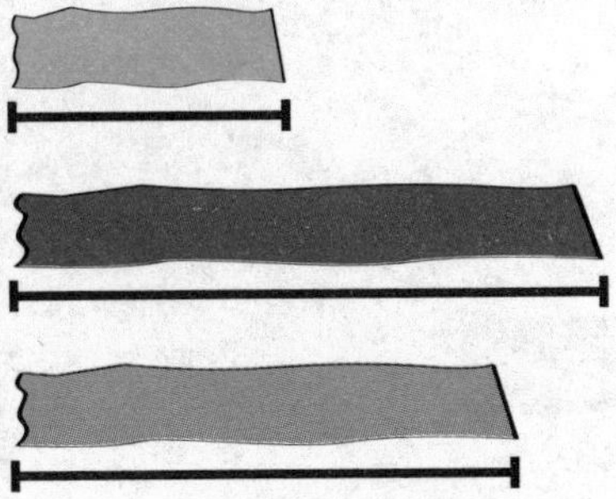

**HOME ACTIVITY** Give your child three household objects of different lengths (such as a remote control, a pencil, and a spoon). Ask him or her to put them in order from longest to shortest.

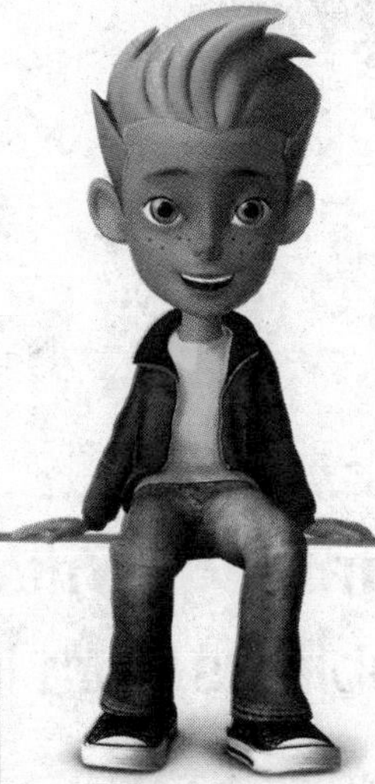

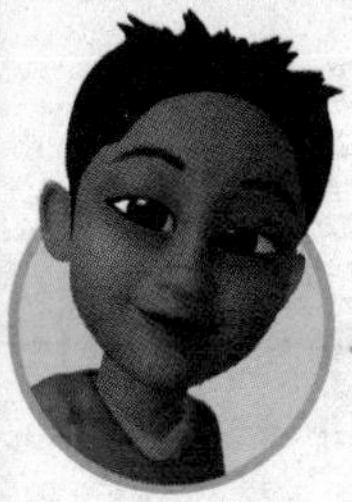

Write the number of the longest object.
Then write the number of the shortest object.

**1.** 1: 2: 3:

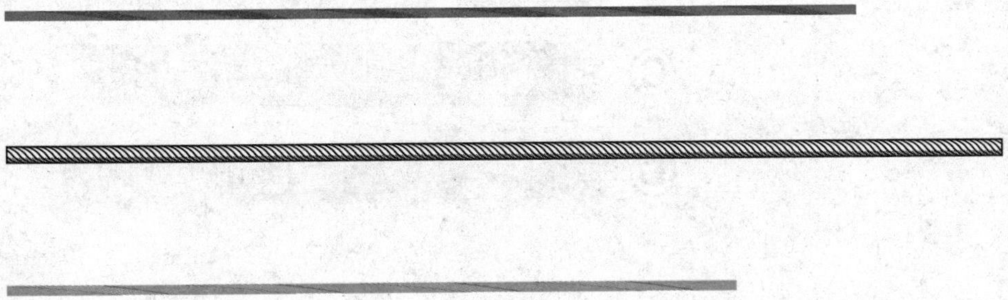

Longest: ____ Shortest: ____

**2.** 1: 2: 3:

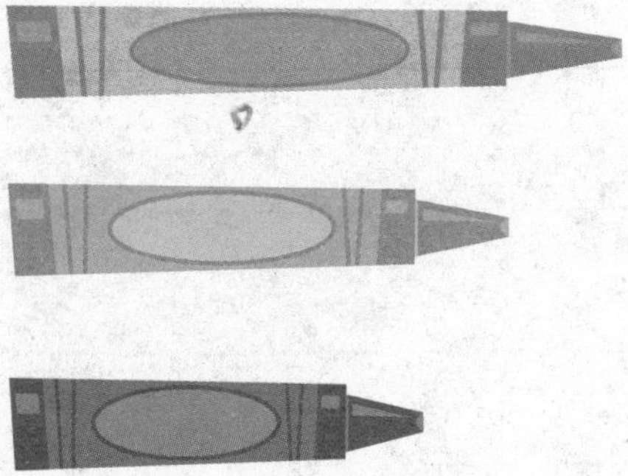

Longest: ____ Shortest: ____

Circle the longest object. Cross out the shortest object.

**3.**

**4.**

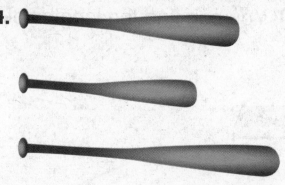

**5. Higher Order Thinking** Write the order of these 3 objects from longest to shortest:

Car   Bike   Airplane

_____

_____

**6. ⊚ Assessment** Which book shown is the longest?

Ⓐ  MATH

Ⓑ  MATH

Ⓒ 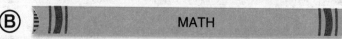 MATH

Ⓓ MATH

Name _____

☆ Solve & Share

How can you find out whether the shoe or the pencil is longer without putting them next to each other? What can you use? Circle the longer object and explain how you found out.

Solve

### Lesson 12-2
### Indirect Measurement

**I can ...**
indirectly compare objects by length.

© **Content Standard** 1.MD.A.1
**Mathematical Practices** MP.1, MP.2, MP.5, MP.7

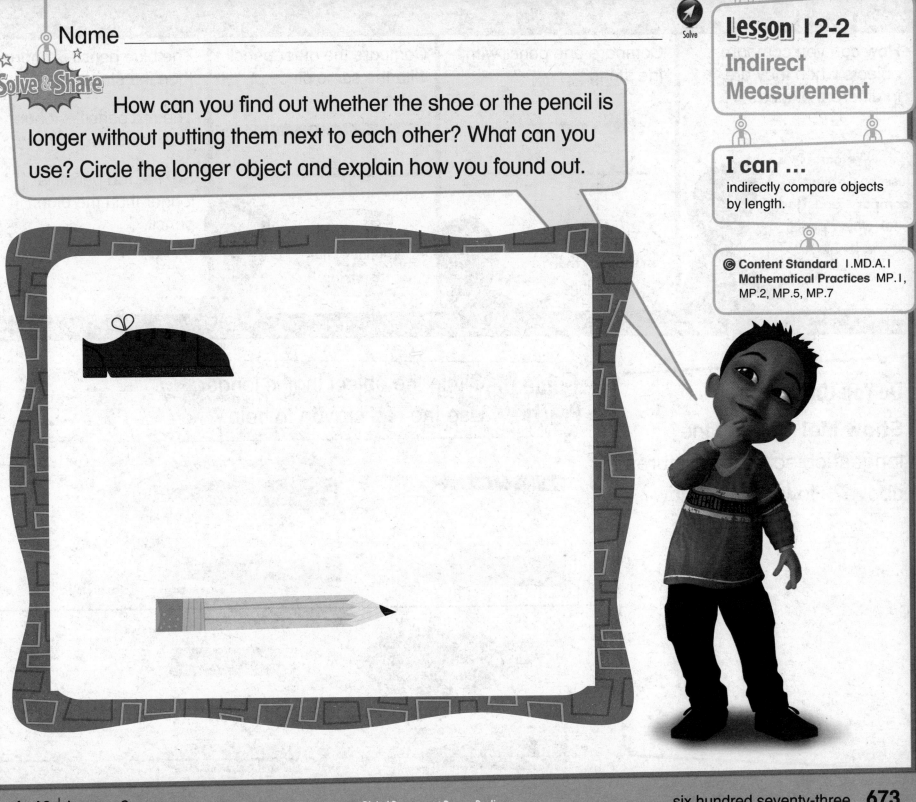

Learn  Glossary

How can you compare objects when they are in different places?

We can use one object to compare and find out which pencil is longer.

Compare one pencil with the string.

This pencil is shorter than the string.

Compare the other pencil with the same piece of string.

This pencil is longer than the string.

The blue pencil is shorter than the string.

The red pencil is longer than the string.

So, the red pencil is longer than the blue pencil.

**Do You Understand?**

**Show Me!** What is the longest object in the pictures above? How do you know?

☆ **Guided** ☆ **Practice** Circle the object that is longer. Use the **red** crayon to help.

1.

2.

© Pearson Education, Inc. 1

Name _____

**Independent Practice**    Circle the object that is longer.
Use the orange string to help.

3.    **frog**                    **leaf**

_____                 _____

4.    **scissors**              **stapler**

_____              _____

5.    **book**              **toothpaste**

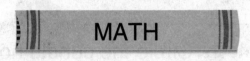
MATH

_____              _____

6.  **toothpaste**              **stapler**

_____              _____

7. **Higher Order Thinking** Use the objects in Items 5 and 6 to fill in the blanks.

The book is longer than the _____.

The toothpaste is longer than the _____.

So, the book is _____ than the stapler.

8. © **MP.1 Make Sense** Use the clues to figure out the name of each dog. Write the name under the correct dog.

**Clues**
- Tango is taller than Bongo.
- Turbo is shorter than Bongo.

What's my plan for solving the problem? How can I check that my answer makes sense?

Bongo

Turbo

Tango

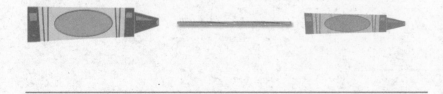

_____   _____   _____

9. **Higher Order Thinking** Josh has two crayons and a piece of string. Explain how he can compare to determine which is the longer crayon without putting the crayons together.

_____

_____

_____

10. © **Assessment** Circle the candle holder that is the longest. Use the **blue** string to help.

Name _____

Help   Tools   Games

**Another Look!** You can compare the lengths of 2 objects without putting them next to each other.

I can use the table to tell if the couch or the bookcase is longer.

The couch is longer than the table.   The bookcase is shorter than the table.

That means the couch is _longer_ than the bookcase.

**HOME ACTIVITY** Review the meanings of *shorter, shortest, longer, longest* with your child. Put 3 different sized objects on the table. Ask your child to tell you which is the shortest and which is the longest. Then ask him or her if one object is longer than another. Then have your child use the words *longer* and *shorter* to compare all 3 objects.

Circle the object that is shorter. Use the **red** string to help.

**1.**

_____   _____

**2.**

SCIENCE

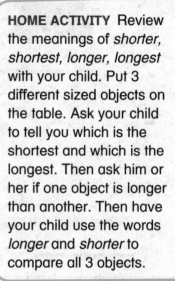

_____   _____

Circle the object that is shorter. Use the **purple** string to help.

**3.**
_____     _____

**4.**
_____     _____

**5.**
_____     _____

**6.**
_____     _____

**7. Higher Order Thinking** Andrea has three candles. Explain how she can use the yellow candle to find out if the red candle is shorter or taller than the blue candle.

_____

_____

**8. ⓒ Assessment** Circle the shape that is longer. Use the **orange** string to help.

_____     _____

Name _____

**Another Look!** You can use smaller objects to measure the length of longer objects. The smaller object will be the length unit.

Use paper clips to measure the length of the book.

**HOME ACTIVITY** Have your child measure the lengths of several small objects. Use paper clips, or other same-size items, as the length unit.

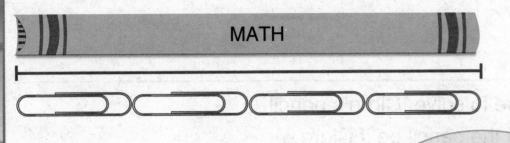

Measure: __4__

Use paper clips that are all the same length. Make sure there are no gaps or overlaps!

 Use paper clips to measure the length.

1.

2.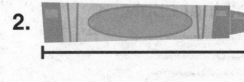

**Topic 12** | Lesson 3   Digital Resources at PearsonRealize.com   six hundred eighty-three **683**

Use paper clips to measure the length.

3.

___

4.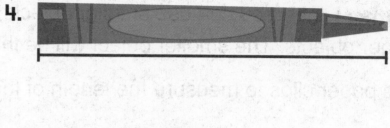

___

5. **Higher Order Thinking** Draw a picture to solve. Clara's pencil is 5 cubes long. About how long would the pencil be if Clara measured it with paper clips? Explain your answer.

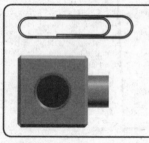

Clara's pencil is about _____ .

6. © **Assessment** Which is **NOT** the correct length of the scissors? Choose all that apply.

☐ 10

☐ 6

☐ 4

☐ 2

© Pearson Education, Inc. 1

## Lesson 12-4

### Continue to Measure Length

**Solve & Share**

Use cubes to measure the length and the height of the poster. Tell whether the poster is longer or taller. How do you know?

**I can ...**
use cubes and other units to compare lengths and heights of objects.

Ⓒ **Content Standards** 1.MD.A.1, 1.MD.A.2
**Mathematical Practices** MP.3, MP.4, MP.6

The poster is _____ than it is _____.

You can measure objects to compare and order their lengths.

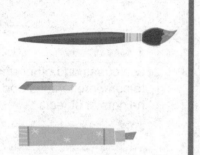

The eraser is about ___3___ long.

The marker is about ___6___ long.

The paintbrush is about ___8___ long.

The paintbrush is longer than the marker and the eraser.

The objects are in order from longest to shortest.

longest ⟶

shortest ⟶

**Do You Understand?**

**Show Me!** How do you know which object is shorter? How do you know which object is longer?

☆ **Guided Practice** ☆ Find each object in your classroom. Measure the length with cubes.

I.

**Bookshelf**

about _____ long

2.

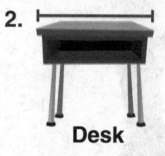

**Desk**

about _____ long

3. The _____ is longer.

© Pearson Education, Inc. 1

**Topic 12 | Lesson 4**

Name _____

## Independent Practice

Find each object in your classroom.
Use cubes to measure how tall it is.

**4.**

| August 2010 |
|---|
| Sunday | Monday | Tuesday | Wednesday | Thursday | Friday | Saturday |
| 1 | 2 | 3 | 4 | 5 | 6 | 7 |
| 8 | 9 | 10 | 11 | 12 | 13 | 14 |
| 15 | 16 | 17 | 18 | 19 | 20 | 21 |
| 22 | 23 | 24 | 25 | 26 | 27 | 28 |
| 29 | 30 | 31 | | | | |

**Calendar**

about _____  tall

**5.**

**Table**

about _____  tall

**6.**

**Chair**

about _____  tall

**7.**

**Trash can**

about _____ tall

Use your measurements above to answer Item 8.

**8. Number Sense** Order the objects from shortest to tallest.

_____  _____  _____  _____

**shortest**                                    **tallest**

9. © **MP.4 Model** Draw a line that is longer than 2 cubes but shorter than 6 cubes. Then use cubes to measure.

My line is about _____ 🔲 long.

10. © **MP.4 Model** Draw a tower that is taller than 3 cubes but shorter than 6 cubes. Then use cubes to measure.

My tower is about _____ 🔲 tall.

11. **Higher Order Thinking** For Item 9, could you have more than one correct answer? Explain.

_____

_____

_____

12. © **Assessment** Measure the green line. Write the number.

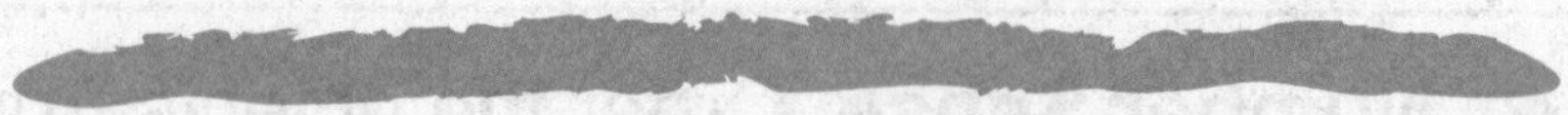

The green line is _____ 🔲 long.

Name _____

**Another Look!** You can use different objects, such as pennies, to measure.

Measure the length of each object using pennies.

4 is the greater number, so the duck is the longer object.

**HOME ACTIVITY**
One penny is about $\frac{3}{4}$-inch long/tall. Work with your child to find an object that is approximately 1 penny long or 1 penny tall. Repeat for 2–5 pennies.

about __4__  long

about __2__  long

Find each object in your house. Measure the length with pennies.

1.

**Shoe**

about _____  long

2.

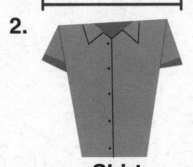

**Shirt**

about _____  long

3.

**Spoon**

about _____ long

Find each object in your house. Measure the length with pennies.

**4.**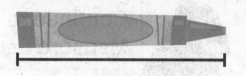

**5.**

**6.**

about _____  long

about _____  long

about _____  tall

**7. Higher Order Thinking** Which of the objects above is the longest? Which is the shortest? Explain how you know.

_____

_____

_____

_____

_____

**8. © Assessment** Measure the height of the rectangle. Write the number.

The rectangle is _____  tall.

Name _____

**Solve & Share**

Which tool or tools would you use to measure the length of the ribbon? Tell why.

Measure the ribbon. Then circle the tools you used.

**I can ...**
choose an appropriate tool and use it to measure a given object.

© Mathematical Practices
MP.5. Also MP.3, MP.8
Content Standard 1.MD.A.2

**Measure**

about _____

**Thinking Habits**
Which tools can I use?

Is there a different tool I could use?

How can you measure an object that is **not** straight?

**Which tools can I use?**

I can use paper clips, cubes, string, or more than one tool!

You can straighten the string and then measure its length with cubes.

The snake is about 5 cubes long.

---

**Do You Understand?**

**Show Me!** Why might you need more than one tool to measure the length of a curvy object?

☆ **Guided Practice** ☆  Circle whether you need just cubes or string and cubes to measure each object. Then measure.

1. cubes          (string and cubes)

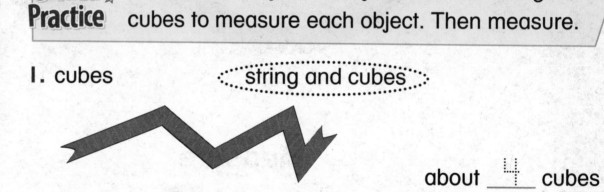

about __4__ cubes

---

2. cubes          string and cubes

about _____ cubes

© Pearson Education, Inc. 1          **Topic 12** | Lesson 5

Tools   Assessment

**Independent Practice**

Circle whether you need just cubes or string and cubes to measure each object. Then measure.

3. cubes                string and cubes

____ cubes

4. cubes                string and cubes

____ cubes

5. cubes                string and cubes

____ cubes

6. cubes                string and cubes

____ cubes

# Math Practices and Problem Solving

### Hanging Bracelets

Kate needs to hang these bracelets in order from shortest to longest.

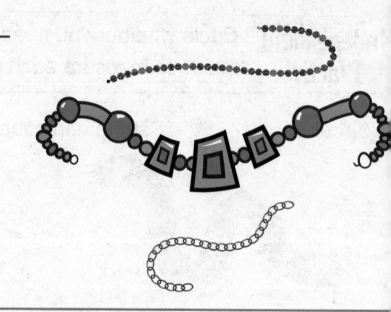

7. **MP.5 Use Tools** Circle the set of tools that Kate should use to measure.

cubes                                    cubes and string

8. **MP.3 Explain** Explain why the tools you chose will give the most accurate measurement.

_____

_____

_____

_____

9. **MP.5 Use Tools** Measure each bracelet. Then write the colors of the bracelets in order from shortest to longest.

_____ , _____ , _____

Name _____

**Another Look!** First use string to measure the ribbon.

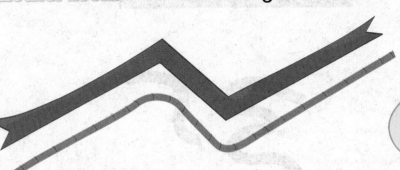

Then use paper clips to measure the string.

The string measures 4 paper clips long.

So, the ribbon is about ___4___ paper clips long.

A string is a good tool to use when you measure an object that isn't straight.

**HOME ACTIVITY** Place a shoelace or piece of string on the table in a curved position (not straight). Ask your child to use cubes (or objects of similar size) to measure the length of the string without straightening it. Then straighten the string and ask your child to measure again. Discuss the difference in the measurements and the reason for this difference.

Circle whether you need just paper clips or string and paper clips to measure each object. Then measure.

1. paper clips      string and paper clips

_____

_____ paper clips

2. paper clips      string and paper clips

_____ paper clips

**Race Courses**

Pete ran races on 3 different courses. Help him put the courses in order from shortest to longest.

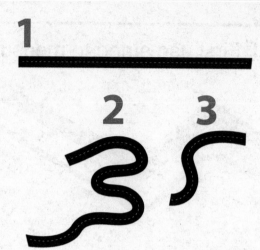

3. **MP.5 Use Tools** Which tools would you use to measure each race course? Would you use the same tools to measure each course? Explain your choice.

_____

_____

_____

4. **MP.3 Explain** Explain why the tools you chose will give the most accurate measurement.

_____

_____

_____

5. **MP.5 Use Tools** Measure each course. Then write the numbers of the courses in order from shortest to longest.

_____ , _____ , _____

Name _____

Find a Match

Find a partner. Point to a clue. Read the clue.

Look below the clues to find a match. Write the clue letter in the box next to the match.

Find a match for every clue.

**I can ...**
add and subtract within 10.

© Content Standard 1.OA.C.6

**Clues**

| **A** $8 + 1$ | **E** $8 - 1$ |
| **B** $4 + 4$ | **F** $1 + 1$ |
| **C** $8 - 3$ | **G** $4 + 2$ |
| **D** $8 - 7$ | **H** $1 + 3$ |

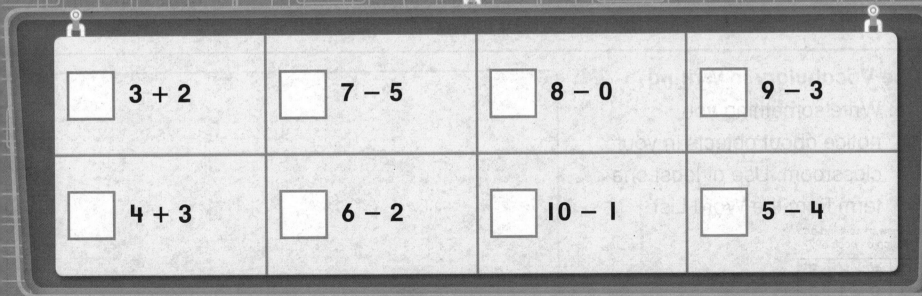

| ☐ $3 + 2$ | ☐ $7 - 5$ | ☐ $8 - 0$ | ☐ $9 - 3$ |
| ☐ $4 + 3$ | ☐ $6 - 2$ | ☐ $10 - 1$ | ☐ $5 - 4$ |

Answers for Find a Match *on next page.*

**A-Z** Glossary

**Word List**
- length
- length unit
- longer
- measure
- shorter
- shortest

## Understand Vocabulary

**1.** Fill in the blank.

I can use _____

to _____ to find

out how long something is.

**2.** Fill in the blank.

The _____

object is the one with the

smallest measurement.

**3.** Circle the lines that
are longer than this
one. _____

_____

_____

**4.** Cross out the
measurement that
is **NOT** shorter
than 19 cubes.

8 cubes

32 cubes

14 cubes

**5.** Cross out the tool that
can **NOT** be used to
measure length.

cubes

number chart

cubes and string

## Use Vocabulary in Writing

**6.** Write something you
notice about objects in your
classroom. Use at least one
term from the Word List.

*Answers for* Find a
Match *on page 697*

| D | A | H | E |
|---|---|---|---|
| G | B | F | C |

Name _____

## Set A

You can find the object that is
the longest.

longest

shortest

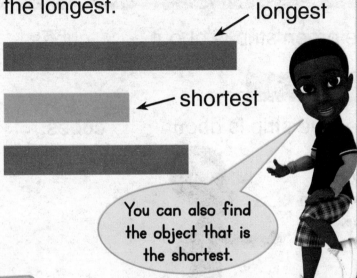

You can also find
the object that is
the shortest.

Circle the longest line in each group.
Draw a box around the shortest line
in each group.

1. _____
   _____
   _____

2. _____
   _____
   _____

## Set B

You can compare the lengths of two
objects that are not lined up next to
each other by using a third object.

The paper clip is shorter than the
eraser. The pencil is longer than the
eraser. So, the pencil is longer than
the paper clip.

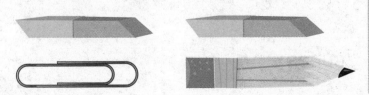

Circle the object that is longer.
Use the red object to help.

3.      MATH

   _____     _____

4. _____     _____

   _____     _____

You can measure the length of an object in cubes.

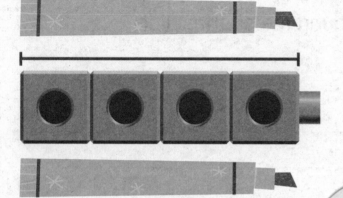

The marker is about ___4___ cubes.

Use cubes to measure.

5.

The green strip is about ____ cubes.

6.

The blue strip is about ____ cubes.

Lay the cubes end to end. Don't leave gaps between them or let them overlap.

**Thinking Habits**

Use Tools

What tool can I use to help solve the problem?

Can I use a different tool? Why or why not?

Choose the tool or tools you can use to measure the object. Then measure the length.

7. cubes      cubes and string

____ cubes

Name _____

1. Circle the tool or tools you would use to measure the length of the picture. Then explain why you chose that tool or tools.

cubes                    string and cubes

_____
_____
_____
_____

---

2. Which word describes the red line?

shortest    middle    tallest    longest

A    B    C    D

3. Use cubes to measure the height of the notebook.

_____  high

**4.** Use cubes to measure the length of the feather.

Ⓐ 2

Ⓒ 4

Ⓑ 6

Ⓓ 8

**5.** Measure the blue, red, and yellow lines with cubes. Which sentences are true about the lines? Choose all that apply.

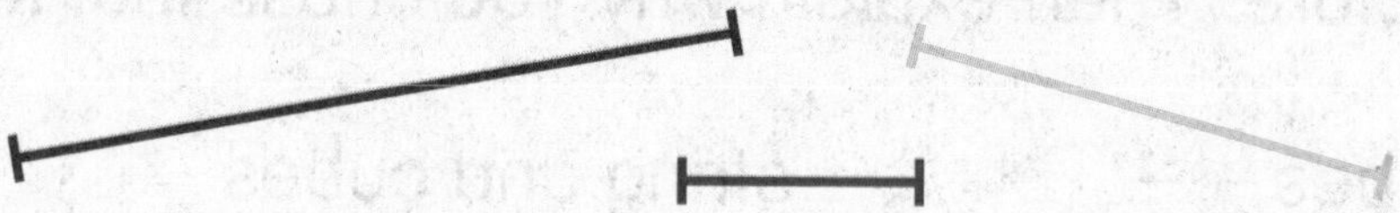

☐ The blue line is shortest.

☐ The red line is shortest.

☐ The blue line is longer than the yellow line.

☐ The yellow line is longer than the blue line.

Circle the object that is shorter. Use the red object to help.

**6.**

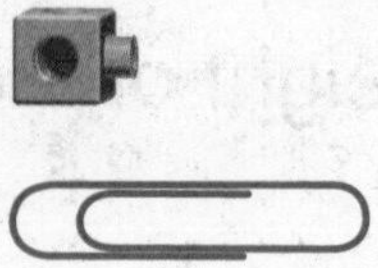

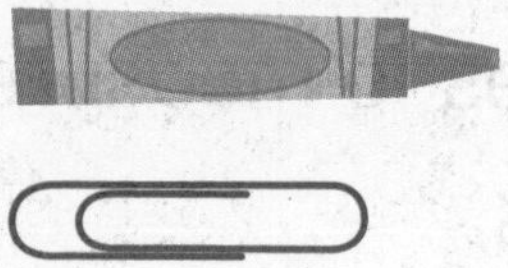

**7.**

**8.** Tom measures the shoe with paper clips. Did Tom measure correctly? Explain.

_____

_____

_____

© Pearson Education, Inc. I

Name _____

## School Supplies

Sally uses many different supplies at school.

1. Which pencil is the longest?
   Circle that color.
   Which pencil is the shortest?
   Cross out that color.

   yellow           red           blue

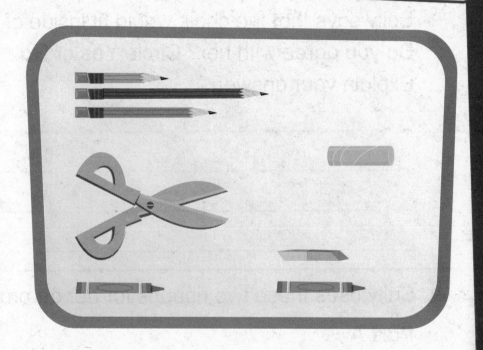

2. Which object is longer? Circle that object. Use the orange object to help.

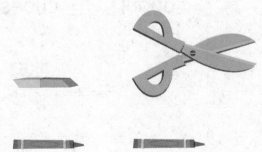

**3.** Use cubes. Measure the length of the chalk.                    _____ cubes

Sally says that the chalk would fit inside of a box that is 6 cubes long.
Do you agree with her? Circle **Yes** or **No**.          **Yes**          **No**
Explain your answer.

_____

_____

_____

_____

---

**4.** Sally uses these two ribbons for her art project.

| **Part A** | **Part B** |
|---|---|
| Use string and cubes to measure the length of each ribbon. | How much longer is the purple ribbon than the pink ribbon? |

about _____ cubes        about _____ cubes

about _____ cubes longer

Digital Resources

Solve   Learn   Glossary

Tools   Assessment   Help   Games

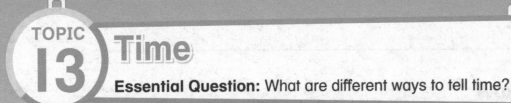

Musical instruments can make many different sounds.

Almost all of these sounds are made when some part of the instrument vibrates.

Wow! Let's do this project and learn more.

**Math and Science Project:** The Sound of Vibration

**Find Out** Talk to friends and relatives about the sounds that different musical instruments make. Ask them if they know what part of the instrument vibrates to make the sound.

**Journal: Make a Book** Show what you found out. In your book, also:

• Draw pictures of different musical instruments.

• Circle or highlight the part of the instrument that vibrates to make a sound.

Name _____

# Review What You Know

## Vocabulary

**1. Count** to find the missing numbers.

28, 29, ____, ____,

32, ____, 34, ____

**2.** Circle the number in the **ones** place.

1 2

**3.** Write the missing numbers to complete the **pattern**.

| Tens | Ones |
|------|------|
| 3 | 3 |
| | |
| 1 | |
| | 33 |

## Counting

**4.** Count by 1s to write the missing numbers.

47, 48, ____, ____,

____, 52, 53, ____

**5.** Count by 10s to write the missing numbers.

____, 20, 30, ____, ____, ____

## Use Tools to Count

**6.** Use what you know about counting on a hundred chart to fill in the missing numbers.

| 31 | 32 | 33 | 34 | | 36 | 37 | 38 | 39 | |
|----|----|----|----|----|----|----|----|----|----|
| 41 | 42 | 43 | 44 | | 46 | 47 | 48 | 49 | |
| 51 | 52 | 53 | 54 | | 56 | 57 | 58 | 59 | |

706 seven hundred six    © Pearson Education, Inc. 1    Topic 13

# My Word Cards

Study the words on the front of the card.
Complete the activity on the back.

A-Z
Glossary

## hour hand

hour hand

## hour

An **hour** is 60 minutes.

2:00

## minute hand

minute hand

## minute

60 **minutes** is 1 hour.

## o'clock

8:00

8 o'clock

## half hour

A **half hour** is 30 minutes.

1:30

# My Word Cards

Use what you know to complete the sentences.
Extend learning by writing your own sentence using each word.

The _____

_____ is the

long hand on a clock.

---

There are 60 minutes in

I _____.

---

The _____

_____ is the

short hand on a clock.

---

There are 30 minutes in a

_____

_____.

---

3:00 is read as

3 _____.

---

There are

60 _____

in I hour.

Name _Aiden_

**Solve & Share**

Draw a picture to show how you would tell time without clocks.

Then tell a partner whether we need clocks or don't need clocks.

**I can ...**
tell time to the hour.

© **Content Standard** I.MD.B.3
**Mathematical Practices** MP.1, MP.5, MP.6, MP.7

The short hand is the **hour hand**.
The hour hand tells us what **hour** it is.

hour hand

The long hand is the **minute hand**.
The minute hand points to the **minute**.

minute hand

When the minute hand points to 12, we say **o'clock**.

This clock shows 3 o'clock.

The hour hand is on 3. The minute hand is on 12.

## Do You Understand?

**Show Me!** How is the hour hand different from the minute hand?

## ☆ Guided Practice ☆ Write the time shown on each clock.

1.

hour hand: _4_

minute hand: _12_

_4_ o'clock

2.

hour hand: ____

minute hand: ____

____ o'clock

3.

hour hand: ____

minute hand: ____

____ o'clock

Name _____

**ndependent Practice** ☆  Draw the hour and minute hands to show the time.

**4.**

10 o'clock

**5.**

2 o'clock

**6.**

11 o'clock

**7.**

12 o'clock

**8.**

6 o'clock

**9.**

1 o'clock

**10.**

5 o'clock

**11.**

8 o'clock

**12. Higher Order Thinking** Write a time.

Draw the hour and minute hands to show the time.

Draw a picture to show an activity you do at that time.

_____ o'clock

13. © **MP.7 Look for Patterns** Sarah wakes up at 7 o'clock. Draw the hands on the clock to show 7 o'clock.

14. **Math and Science** Each string on a guitar makes a different sound when it vibrates. Joe starts tuning his guitar at 9 o'clock. It takes him one hour to finish. What time does he finish?

_____ o'clock

15. **Higher Order Thinking** Karen starts playing soccer one hour after 5 o'clock. Draw the hour and minute hands on the clock to show what time Karen starts playing soccer.

Then write a sentence about an activity you might do at that time.

_____

_____

16. © **Assessment** Bill likes to read after 3 o'clock and before 5 o'clock. Which clock shows the time Bill might read?

Ⓐ

Ⓑ

Ⓒ

Ⓓ

Name _____

Help   Tools   Games

**Another Look!** You can use the hands on a clock to tell time. The short hand is the hour hand. The long hand is the minute hand.

minute hand

hour hand

The hour hand points to 6.

The minute hand points to 12.

It is 6 o'clock.

The hour hand points to _3_.

The minute hand points to _12_.

It is _3_ o'clock.

**HOME ACTIVITY** Using an analog clock in your home, help your child make a list of activities they do on a given day. Have him or her write the time that each activity begins.

Write the time shown on each clock.

1.

hour hand: _____

minute hand: _____

_____ o'clock

2.

hour hand: _____

minute hand: _____

_____ o'clock

3.

hour hand: _____

minute hand: _____

_____ o'clock

Draw hour hands and minute hands to show the time.

**4.**

10 o'clock

**5.**

2 o'clock

**6.**

11 o'clock

**7.**

3 o'clock

**8.**

9 o'clock

**9.**

6 o'clock

Solve each problem below.

**10. Higher Order Thinking** Write a good time for eating lunch. Then draw an hour hand and a minute hand to show the time.

_____ o'clock

**11.** Ⓒ **Assessment** Every Saturday, Rachel wakes up after 6 o'clock and before 9 o'clock. Which tells the time Rachel might wake up every Saturday?

Ⓐ 2 o'clock

Ⓑ 4 o'clock

Ⓒ 5 o'clock

Ⓓ 8 o'clock

© Pearson Education, Inc. 1

**Topic 13** | Lesson

Solve

**Solve & Share**

Both of the clocks show the same time. Tell what time is shown. Then write one way the clocks are alike and one way they are different.

**I can ...**

tell time to the hour using 2 different types of clock.

© **Content Standard** I.MD.B.3
**Mathematical Practices** MP.2, MP.6, MP.7, MP.8

9:00

**Alike**

**Different**

____ o'clock

_____          _____
_____          _____
_____          _____
_____          _____

I eat breakfast at 7 o'clock.

This clock shows 7 o'clock.

This clock shows 7 o'clock another way.

 7:00

7 tells the hour. 00 tells the minutes.

7 o'clock is the same as 7:00.

 7:00

## Do You Understand?

**Show Me!** Do the clocks show the same time? Explain.

 8:00

☆ **Guided Practice** ☆  Draw the hands on the clock face. Then write the time on the other clock.

1.   3:00

3 o'clock

2.   :

5 o'clock

3.   :

12 o'clock

4.   :

11 o'clock

© Pearson Education, Inc. 1
**Topic 13** | Lesson 2

Name _____

## Independent Practice

Draw the hands on the clock face.
Then write the time on the other clock.

**5.**

2 o'clock

**6.**

4 o'clock

**7.**

6 o'clock

**8.**

9 o'clock

**9.**

10 o'clock

**10.**

1 o'clock

Think about how hands move on a clock to help solve the problem.

**11. Number Sense** Mary writes a pattern.
Then she erases some of the times.
Write the missing times.          6:00, 8:00, _____ : _____, 12:00, _____ : _____

**12.** ⓒ **MP.2 Reasoning** Raul starts riding his bike at 1:00. He rides for 1 hour. What time does Raul stop? Draw the hands on the clock face. Then write the time on the other clock.

**13.** Ⓐ-ⓩ **Vocabulary** Lucy reads for 1 **hour**. She stops reading at 10:00. What time did Lucy start reading? Draw the hands on the clock face. Then write the **hour** Lucy starts reading.

_____ o'clock

**14. Higher Order Thinking** David goes to bed 2 hours before his mother. David's mother goes to bed at 11:00.

Write the time David goes to bed on the clock.

**15.** ⓒ **Assessment** Maribel washes dishes after 6:00 and before 9:00. Which clocks show a time Maribel might wash dishes? Choose all that apply.

Name _____

Help    Tools    Games

**Another Look!** Both clocks show the same time.

4 tells the hour.

00 tells the minutes.

Both clocks show 4 o'clock.

_7_ tells the hour.

_00_ tells the minutes.

Both clocks show _7_ o'clock.

**HOME ACTIVITY** Use a digital clock in your home to help your child practice telling time. When your child is doing an activity on the hour, ask him or her to tell you the time. Repeat with other times and other activities.

Draw the hands on the clock face.
Then write the time on the other clock.

**1.**

3 o'clock

**2.**

7 o'clock

**3.**

10 o'clock

Draw lines to match the clocks that show the same time.

**4.**

 1:00     3:00

**5.**

 12:00     9:00

**6.**

5:00    6:00

**7. Higher Order Thinking** Write a good time for eating dinner.

Draw hands on the clock face to show the time. Then write the time on the other clock.

_____ o'clock

**8. © Assessment** Look at the time on the clock face. Which clocks below do **NOT** show the same time? Choose all that apply.

 10:00    8:00    7:00    4:00

□            □            □            □

© Pearson Education, Inc. I

Name _____

**Solve & Share**

The red clock shows a time to the hour. The blue clock is missing its minute hand.

Draw the minute hand on the blue clock so the clock shows a half hour later. Tell why you think you are right.

**I can ...**
tell time to the half hour.

© **Content Standard** 1.MD.B.3
**Mathematical Practices** MP.2, MP.3, MP.6, MP.7

An hour is 60 minutes. A half hour is 30 minutes.

When the minute hand is on 6, we can say 30 or half past the hour.

The hour hand is halfway between the 2 and 3.

It is half past 2 or 2:30.

2:30

## Do You Understand?

**Show Me!** Why is the hour hand between 6 and 7 when it is 6:30?

## ☆Guided☆ Practice

Write the numbers to complete each sentence. Then write the time on the other clock.

1. The hour hand is between

   _7_ and _8_.

   The minute hand is on _6_.

7:30

2. The hour hand is between

   ____ and ____.

   The minute hand is on ____.

Name _____

☆ **Independent Practice** ☆  Write the time shown on each clock.

**3.**

**4.**

**5.**

Look at the pattern. Write the missing times.

**6.** 6:00, 6:30, 7:00, _____, 8:00, _____, _____

**7.** 2:30, 3:30, _____, 5:30, _____, _____

**8. Higher Order Thinking** Carlos plays basketball for 30 minutes each day. He always starts playing at half past an hour. Write times he might start and stop playing basketball. Draw the hands on each clock face to show the times.

**START**

__ : __

**STOP**

__ : __

9. ⓒ **MP.6 Be Precise** Sandy walks her dog at 3:00. She walks for 30 minutes. What time does Sandy stop walking her dog? Draw the hands on the clock face. Write the time on the other clock.

10. ⓒ **MP.6 Be Precise** Robin gets to school at 9:00. Her math class starts 30 minutes later. What time does Robin's math class start? Draw the hands on the clock face. Write the time on the other clock.

11. **Higher Order Thinking** Show 8:00 on the first clock. On the second clock, show the time 30 minutes later. Is the hour hand still on 8? Explain.

_____

_____

_____

12. ⓒ **Assessment** Which clock below shows the same time as the clock face?

| 12:30 | 1:30 | 2:30 | 3:30 |

Ⓐ     Ⓑ     Ⓒ     Ⓓ

Name _____

Help  Tools  Games

**Another Look!** Clocks can tell us the time to the half hour.

A half hour is 30 minutes.

The hour hand is between
7 and 8.
The minute hand is on 6.
It is 7:30.

The hour hand is between
__11__ and __12__.

The minute hand is on __6__.
It is __11:30__.

**HOME ACTIVITY** Using an analog clock, have your child practice telling the time to the half hour. If possible, have him or her move the hands on the clock to tell the time you say. For example, say, "Show me 6:30." Have your child write the time on a sheet of paper after telling the time.

Complete the sentences. Then write the time on the other clock.

**1.**

The hour hand is between _____ and _____.
The minute hand is on _____.
It is _____.

**2.**

The hour hand is between _____ and _____.
The minute hand is on _____.
It is _____.

3. © **MP.3 Explain** It takes Vanessa a half hour to walk to the library. She leaves her house at 5:00. What time does she get to the library?

Write the time on the clock.
Then explain how you solved.

_____

_____

_____

4. **Algebra** Kirk stirs his soup at 1:00. He started cooking the soup 30 minutes earlier. What time did Kirk start cooking his soup? Draw the hands on the clock face and write the time.

_____ : _____

5. **Higher Order Thinking** Write about something you do a half hour before bedtime. Write the time on the clock. Draw the hands on the clock face to show the time.

_____

_____

6. © **Assessment** Which shows the same time as the clock face?

8:30            8:00            7:30            6:30

Ⓐ              Ⓑ              Ⓒ              Ⓓ

© Pearson Education, Inc. 1

Name _____

Solve & Share

Noel has a music lesson at 3:30. At 4:30, he goes to the library. He gets ready at 5:00 so he can have dinner at 5:30. After dinner ends at 6:00, he plays a game. How can you organize this information in a schedule?

**I can ...**
use reasoning to tell and write time.

© Mathematical Practices MP.2
Also MP.3, MP.4, MP.8
Content Standard I.MD.B.3

## Afternoon Schedule

| Time | Activity |
|------|----------|
|      |          |
|      |          |
|      |          |
|      |          |
|      |          |

**Thinking Habits**

What do the numbers stand for?

How are the numbers in the problem related?

Mr. Diaz starts to read a story halfway between 8:00 and 9:00. What time does Mr. Diaz start the story? Show the hands on the clock.

| Mr. Diaz's Class Schedule | |
|---|---|
| **Time** | **Activity** |
| 8:00 | Reading |
| 9:00 | Math |
| 10:00 | Recess |
| 10:30 | Art |
| 11:30 | Lunch |

**How can I make sense of the question?**

What does "halfway" mean?

**What is my thinking?**

The time between 8:00 and 9:00 is one hour, or 60 minutes. A half hour is 30 minutes.

8:30 is halfway between 8:00 and 9:00. I can look back at the table to see if my answer makes sense.

## Do You Understand?

**Show Me!** What happens 1 hour after Art begins? Explain how you know.

☆ **Guided Practice** ☆ Use Mr. Diaz's Class Schedule above to answer the questions. Circle the activity that starts at the time shown. Then explain your reasoning.

1.

Recess

Art

Reading

_____

_____

2.

Art

Recess

Lunch

_____

_____

© Pearson Education, Inc. 1

Topic 13 | Lesson 4

Name _____

Tools  Assessment

**Independent Practice** ☆ Use the Nature Trip Schedule to answer the questions.

3. Which activity do children do just before the Bird Watch?
Explain your reasoning.

_____

_____

4. Which activity or activities do children do after Lunch?
Explain your reasoning.

_____

_____

5. Which activity starts at the time shown?
Explain your reasoning.

_____

_____

| Nature Trip Schedule | |
|---|---|
| **Time** | **Activity** |
| 10:00 | Walk |
| 11:00 | Bird Watch |
| 12:00 | Lunch |
| 12:30 | Make a Birdhouse |
| 1:30 | Pick Flowers |

6. 🅰🆉 **Vocabulary** Circle the time that shows a **half hour** past 3:00.

2:00          3:00          3:30          4:00

# Math Practices and Problem Solving

**Visiting the City** Andrew's family takes a day trip to the city.

Help him solve problems using the Family Schedule.

| Family Schedule | |
|---|---|
| **Time** | **Activity** |
| 10:00 | Museum |
| 12:30 | Aquarium |
| 2:00 | City Tour |
| 4:30 | C Building |
| 5:30 | Dinner |

7. **MP.4 Model** The minute hand fell off this clock. What time should the clock show when Andrew's family arrives at the Aquarium?

Draw the minute hand and write the time shown.

_____

8. **MP.2 Reasoning** Andrew writes down all the activities his family is doing at 30 minutes after the hour. How many activities did Andrew write? Explain how you found out.

_____

_____

_____

© Pearson Education, Inc. 1

Name _____

**Another Look!** You can use reasoning to solve problems about time.

Mr. K's students can work with a partner for the second half of Writing.

What time can students start working with a partner?

How are the numbers related? How can you use what you know to solve?

Students can start working with a partner at  1:30.

### Class Schedule

| Time | Class |
|------|-------|
| 12:30 | Silent Reading |
| 1:00 | Writing |
| 2:00 | P.E. |

**HOME ACTIVITY** Help your child create a schedule for a typical school day. Ask questions about the schedule, such as, "What time do you eat lunch?" or "What time is a half hour after Math?"

What time is halfway between 1:00 and 2:00? I know 1:00 to 2:00 is 1 hour. I know a half hour is 30 minutes. 30 minutes after 1:00 is 1:30.

Use the schedule above to solve the problems below.

1. Draw the hands on the clock to show when Silent Reading begins.
   Then explain your reasoning.

_____
_____
_____

2. What time is it 30 minutes after P.E. starts?
   Write the correct time on the clock.
   Then explain your reasoning.

_____
_____

© **Performance Assessment**

**Fun Run** Gina's school is hosting a fundraiser for music programs. Can you use the schedule to help solve problems about the fundraiser?

Use your understanding of telling and writing time to solve the problems.

| Fundraiser Schedule | |
| Time | Activity |
| --- | --- |
| 10:00 | Introductions |
| 10:30 | Auction |
| 11:30 | Fun Run |
| 2:00 | Closing Speech |

3. **MP.4 Model** What time do the introductions start at the fundraiser? Write the correct time on the clock to show your answer.

4. **MP.2 Reasoning** Gina drew the hands on this clock to show the time the Closing Speech starts. Is she correct? If not, draw the correct hands on the clock at the right.

© Pearson Education, Inc. 1

Name _____

**Point & Tally**

Find a partner. Get paper and a pencil.

Each partner chooses a different color: light blue or dark blue.

Partner 1 and Partner 2 each point to a black number at the same time. Both partners add those numbers.

If the answer is on your color, you get a tally mark.

Work until one partner gets twelve tally marks.

**I can ...**
add and subtract within 10.

© Content Standard I.OA.C.6

**Partner 1**

| 8 |
| 6 |
| 0 |
| 7 |
| 3 |
| 5 |

| 0 | 6 | 10 | 9 | 3 | 8 |
| 1 | 7 | 2 | 4 | 0 | 5 |

**Tally Marks for Partner 1**

**Tally Marks for Partner 2**

**Partner 2**

| 0 |
| 1 |
| 2 |
| 1 |
| 0 |
| 2 |

**A-Z Glossary**

**Word List**
- half hour
- hour
- hour hand
- minute
- minute hand
- o'clock

## Understand Vocabulary

**1.** Circle the hour hand.

**2.** Circle the minute hand.

**3.** Fill in the blank.
Use a word from the Word List.
30 minutes is a

_____.

**4.** Fill in the blank.
Use a word from the Word List.
In the time 8:30, 8 is the

_____.

**5.** Fill in the blank.
Use a word from the Word List.
In the time 8:30, 30 is the _____.

## Use Vocabulary in Writing

**6.** Tell what time is shown on the clock using a word from the Word List.

**10:00**

© Pearson Education, Inc. 1

Name _____

## Set A

You can draw the hour and minute hands to show the time.

minute hand

hour hand

8 o'clock

When the minute hand points to 12, you say o'clock.

Draw the hour and minute hands to show the time.

1.

3 o'clock

2.

11 o'clock

## Set B

What time does the clock show?

5 shows the hour.
00 shows the minutes.

5:00

5 o'clock

Write the time shown on each clock.

3.

6:00

_____ o'clock

4.

10:00

_____ o'clock

What time do the clocks show?

half past __8__

or __8__ : __30__

Remember: Half past means 30 minutes after the hour.

Write the time shown on each clock.

5.

7:30

half past _____

or _____ : _____

6.

half past _____

or _____ : _____

**Thinking Habits**

Reasoning

What do the numbers stand for?

How are the numbers in the problem related?

Use the schedule to answer the questions.

| Mr. Diaz's Class Schedule | |
|---|---|
| **Time** | **Activity** |
| 8:30 | Reading |
| 9:30 | 1+1= Math |
| 10:30 | Recess |

7. What activity starts 2 hours after Reading?

_____

8. What time does Math begin?

_____ : _____

Name _____

1. Lisa rides her bike after 2 o'clock and before 6 o'clock every Friday. Which clocks show the time Lisa might ride her bike? Choose all that apply.

☐ ☐ ☐ ☐

2. Which clock shows the same time as the clock face?

12:00   1:00   2:00   3:00
Ⓐ        Ⓑ      Ⓒ      Ⓓ

3. Write the time that is shown on the clock face.

:

**4.** How many minutes are in a half hour?

15
Ⓐ

20
Ⓑ

30
Ⓒ

60
Ⓓ

**5.** Write the numbers to complete the sentence.

When Arts and Crafts starts, the hour
hand is between ____ and ____.

| Camp Schedule | |
|---|---|
| **Time** | **Activity** |
| 11:00 | Lunch |
| 12:00 | Swimming |
| 1:30 | Story Time |
| 2:00 | Snack Time |
| 2:30 | Arts and Crafts |

**6.** Draw hands on the clock face to show the
time that Story Time starts.

**7.** Show the same time on both clocks. How do you know you are correct?

_____

_____

_____

_____

© Pearson Education, Inc. 1

Name _____

## A Trip to the Zoo

Carol and her class take a trip to the zoo.
The chart shows their schedule.

| Zoo Schedule | |
|---|---|
| **Time** | **Activity** |
| 9:00 | Bird House |
| 9:30 | Train Ride |
| 10:00 | Large Animals |
| 11:30 | Lunch |
| 12:30 | Dolphin Show |
| 1:00 | Small Animals |

**I.** Show another way to write the time
for each activity.

Large Animals

_____

Train Ride

_____

**2.** Draw the hands on the clock
to show the time for the
Dolphin Show.

**3.** The class left school 30 minutes before
they got to the Bird House.

Draw the hands and write the time on the
clocks to show what time they left school.

**4.** The class will see the Small Animals for 30 minutes.

What time will it be then? Choose a way to show the time.

```



```

The class will be back at school 30 minutes after they finish seeing the Small Animals.

What time will it be then? Choose a way to show the time.

```



```

**5.** Carol says that this clock shows the same time that Lunch starts.

Do you agree with her?

Circle **Yes** or **No**.

Explain your answer.

_____

_____

_____

_____

_____

© Pearson Education, Inc. I

**Topic 13** | Performance Assessment

# Reason with Shapes and Their Attributes

**Essential Question:** How can you define shapes and compose new shapes?

Materials can be made into shapes that help do a job.

Bricks are rectangular prisms. They stack to make buildings!

Wow! Let's do this project and learn more.

## Math and Science Project: Use Shapes to Build

**Find Out** Talk to friends and relatives about everyday objects that have special shapes. Discuss how the shape is important for its use.

**Journal: Make a Book** Show what you found out. In your book, also:

• Draw different buildings using circles, squares, rectangles, cylinders, and rectangular prisms.

• In your drawings, show how shapes can be put together to make new shapes.

Name _____

# Review What You Know

**A-Z Vocabulary**

**1.** Scott **sorted** these shapes. Put an X on the one that does not belong.

**2.** Circle the object that is a **different** shape.

**3.** Circle the **square**.

---

## Same and Different

**4.** Draw a shape that is the same as the one below.

**5.** Draw a shape that is different from the one below.

## Count by 1s

**6.** Write the missing numbers.

1, ____, 3, 4, ____

# My Word Cards

Study the words on the front of the card.
Complete the activity on the back.

## 2-D shapes

 circle

 rectangle

 square

 triangle

## side

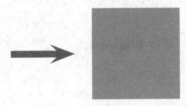

## vertex/vertices

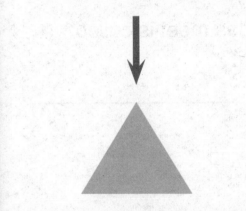

## 3-D shapes

 cone

 cylinder

 sphere

 cube

 rectangular prism

## flat surfaces

## edges

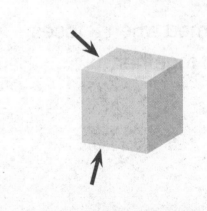

# My Word Cards

Use what you know to complete the sentences.
Extend learning by writing your own sentence using each word.

The point where two

sides meet is called

a _____.

A square has

4 _____

that are equal.

Circles and squares are

_____

_____.

An _____

is formed when 2 faces
come together.

A cylinder has

2 _____

_____.

Cubes, cones, cylinders,
and spheres are

_____

_____.

© Pearson Education, Inc. 1

# My Word Cards

Study the words on the front of the card. Complete the activity on the back.

A-Z
Glossary

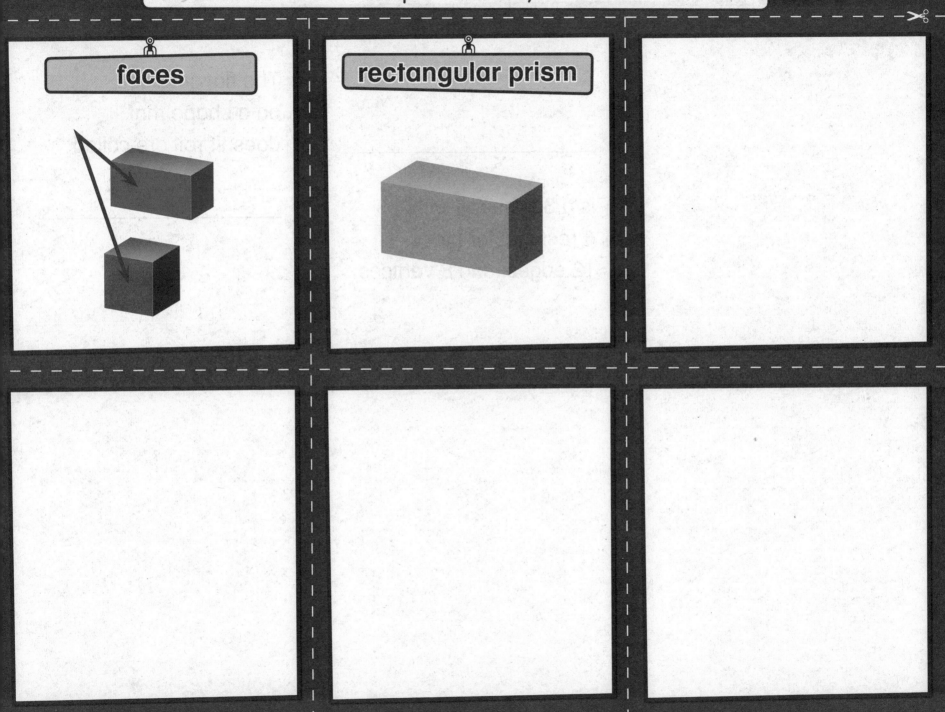

**faces**

**rectangular prism**

A _____

_____

is a 3-D shape with
6 rectangular faces,
12 edges, and 8 vertices.

The flat surfaces
on a shape that
doesn't roll are called

_____.

© Pearson Education, Inc. 1

Name _____

**Solve & Share**

Draw an object from your classroom that matches each shape below.

How do you know that the shape you drew is the same as the one on the page?

**I can ...**
use attributes to match shapes.

© Content Standard 1.G.A.1
Mathematical Practices MP.6, MP.7, MP.8

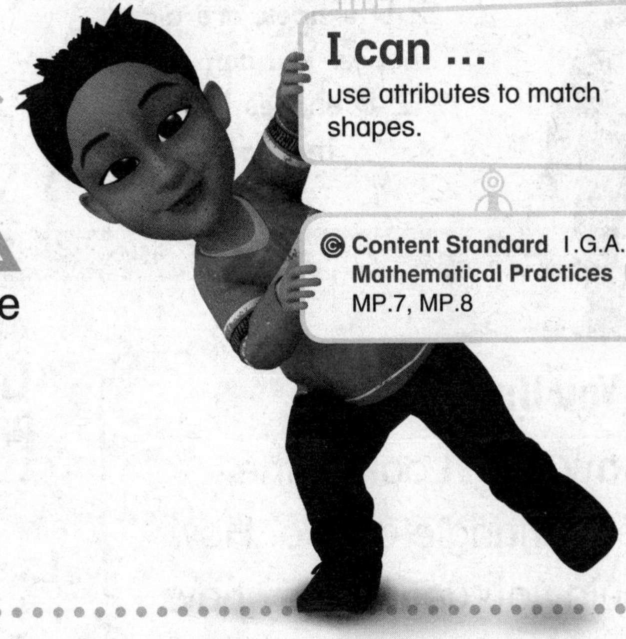

Square

Circle

Triangle

Rectangle

Hexagon

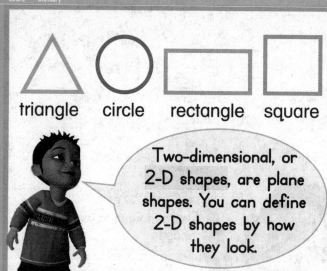

triangle    circle    rectangle    square

Two-dimensional, or 2-D shapes, are plane shapes. You can define 2-D shapes by how they look.

Some 2-D shapes have straight **sides** and some 2-D shapes do not.

3 straight sides

0 straight sides

Some 2-D shapes have corners called **vertices** and some 2-D shapes do not.

3 vertices

0 vertices

2-D shapes are closed. Their sides are all connected.

This is not a triangle. It is not a closed shape with 3 sides.

## Do You Understand?

**Show Me!** Look at the green triangle above. How would you define it by how it looks?

☆ **Guided Practice** ☆   For each shape, tell how many straight sides or vertices, and if it is closed or not.

1.  How many straight sides? __4__
Closed? __Yes__

2.  How many vertices? ____
Closed? ____

3.  How many straight sides? ____
Closed? ____

© Pearson Education, Inc. 1

**Topic 14** | Lesson 1

Tools  Assessment

## Independent Practice   Draw each shape.

**4.** Draw a closed shape with 3 vertices.

**5.** Draw a closed shape with 0 straight sides.

**6.** Draw a closed shape with more than 3 vertices.

**7.** Circle the closed shapes.

**8. Higher Order Thinking** Look at the shapes in each group. Explain how the shapes are sorted.

_____

_____

_____

**Group 1**

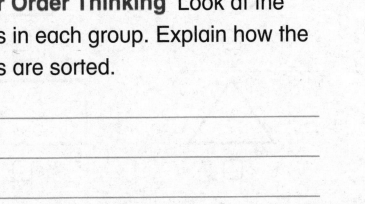

**Group 2**

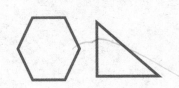

**9.** © **MP.6 Be Precise** Circle 3 shapes that have the same number of vertices and sides.

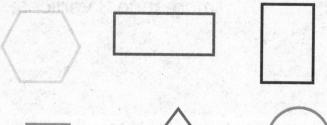

**10.** © **MP.6 Be Precise** Circle 3 shapes that do **NOT** have any vertices.

**11. Higher Order Thinking** Think about a 2-D shape. Write a riddle about the shape for a partner to solve.

_____

_____

_____

_____

**12.** © **Assessment** I have 4 vertices. My sides are equal. Which shape or shapes can I **NOT** be? Choose all that apply.

© Pearson Education, Inc. 1

Name _____

Help    Tools    Games

**Another Look!** You can sort shapes by the number of straight sides and vertices. A shape is closed if the sides are connected.

Tell if the shape is closed or not. Then count the straight sides and vertices.

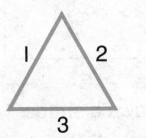 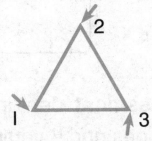

A triangle is a closed shape with 3 straight sides and 3 vertices.

Closed? __Yes__ A square has __4__ straight sides and __4__ vertices.

**HOME ACTIVITY** Draw a square, a rectangle, a triangle, and a circle. Have your child tell how many straight sides and how many vertices each shape has.

For each shape, tell if it is closed or not. Then tell how many sides and vertices it has.

1.

Closed?_____ A circle has _____ straight sides and _____ vertices.

2.

Closed?_____ A rectangle has _____ straight sides and _____ vertices.

3.
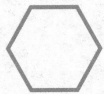
Closed?_____ A hexagon has _____ straight sides and _____ vertices.

Topic 14 | Lesson 1          Digital Resources at PearsonRealize.com          seven hundred fifty-one **751**

Draw each shape.

**4.** Draw a shape with more than 3 sides.

**5.** Draw a shape with 4 vertices.

**6.** Draw a shape with no vertices.

**7. Higher Order Thinking** A rhombus is a closed shape with 4 equal sides and 4 vertices. Circle the shape that is not a rhombus. Explain how you know.

_____

_____

_____

**8. © Assessment** Jen draws a shape with 4 sides and 4 vertices. Which could be Jen's shape? Choose all that apply.

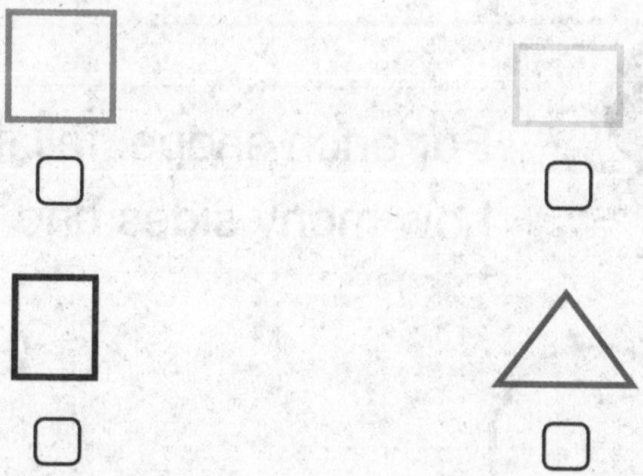

© Pearson Education, Inc. 1

Name _____

Solve

Lesson 14-2

Defining and
Non-Defining
Attributes of
2-D Shapes

**Solve & Share**

Are all these figures the same kind of shape? Explain how you know.

_____

_____

_____

Are these all the same kind of shape?

Shapes are defined by the number of straight sides and vertices, and whether they are closed or not.

This is a closed shape. It has 4 vertices and 2 pairs of sides that are the same length. This shape is a rectangle.

Shapes are not defined by color.

These shapes are all blue. But I see a rectangle, a circle, and a hexagon.

Shapes are not defined by size or position.

These are all rectangles!

## Do You Understand?

**Show Me!** Draw 4 hexagons. How do you know they are all hexagons?

## ☆ Guided ☆ Practice

Circle the words that are true for the shape.

1.

All squares:

are blue.

have 4 equal sides.

are closed shapes.

are small.

Name _____

**Independent Practice**    Circle the words that are true for each shape.

2.      All triangles:     have 3 sides.

have 3 equal sides.

are tall.

are orange.

3.      All circles:     are blue.

have 0 vertices.

are small.

have 0 straight sides.

4. **Higher Order Thinking** Tim says
that this is a triangle. Is he correct?
Tell why or why not.

_____

_____

_____

5. © **MP.5 Use Tools**  Do all triangles have equal sides? Circle **Yes** or **No**.

   **Yes      No**

   Choose a tool to show how you know.

6. **Higher Order Thinking**  Jake says both of these shapes are hexagons because they are closed, have 6 straight sides, and are red. Do you agree? Explain.

7. © **Assessment**  Match each shape with the words that describe it.

   Rectangle                    Circle                      Triangle

   3 vertices                   4 vertices                  No sides or vertices

Name _____

**Another Look!** You can use certain features to identify shapes.

How can you tell if a shape is a square?

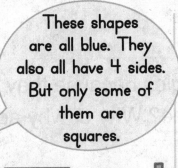

These shapes are all blue. They also all have 4 sides. But only some of them are squares.

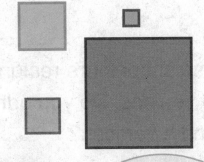

These shapes are all different colors and sizes. But they are all squares.

All squares: have 4 equal sides.

are blue.

are small.

have 4 vertices.

**HOME ACTIVITY** Work with your child to find shapes around the house (such as triangles, squares, and hexagons). Then make lists of defining attributes for each shape. Ask him or her to draw or construct 3 different examples of each shape.

Circle the words that are true for the shape.

1. 

All triangles:    are yellow.       have 3 straight sides.

          are short.        have 3 vertices.

Circle the words that are true for the shape.

2.

All hexagons:     are purple.     have 6 equal sides.

have 6 straight sides.     have 6 vertices.

3. **Higher Order Thinking** Danielle says these shapes are rectangles because they are both tall shapes with 4 straight sides and 4 vertices. Do you agree? Why or why not? What other shapes have 4 straight sides and 4 vertices?

4. © **Assessment** Match each shape with the words that describe it.

Triangle          Square          Hexagon          Circle

4 equal sides     3 vertices      6 sides          No sides or vertices

Name _____

**Solve & Share**

Use the items your teacher gave you to make 2 different rectangles. Tell what makes each shape a rectangle.

**I can ...**
use different materials to make shapes.

© **Content Standard** I.G.A.1
**Mathematical Practices** MP.2, MP.4, MP.5, MP.8

## Rectangle 1            Rectangle 2

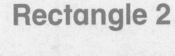

2-D shapes can be made using all kinds of materials.

You have to think about how your shape looks.

I am going to make a triangle. What makes a triangle a triangle?

A triangle has 3 sides and 3 vertices.

This is a triangle, too.

It looks a little different but the shape still has 3 sides and 3 vertices.

## Do You Understand?

**Show Me!** Sue made the shape on the right. Is it also a hexagon? Tell how you know.

☆ **Guided Practice** ☆

Make a square. Use materials your teacher gives you. Glue or tape the square in the box. Explain how you know it is a square.

I.

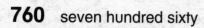

© Pearson Education, Inc. 1

**Topic 14** | Lesson 3

Name _____

Tools  Assessment

## Independent Practice

Use materials your teacher gives you to make each shape. Glue or tape the shape in the box. Explain how you know the shape is correct.

**2.** Make a circle.

**3.** Make a rectangle.

**4. Higher Order Thinking** Carlos made the shapes below. He says they are both squares. Is he correct? Explain.

_____

_____

_____

_____

**Topic 14** | Lesson 3

seven hundred sixty-one  **761**

Draw a picture to solve each problem below. Use pattern blocks to help you.

5. **© MP.2 Reasoning** Sandy makes a closed shape with 4 equal sides. What shape did she make?

_____

Draw the shape Sandy made.

6. **© MP.2 Reasoning** Miguel makes a closed shape with 3 straight sides and 3 vertices. What shape did Miguel make?

_____

Draw the shape Miguel made.

7. **Higher Order Thinking** Use a piece of paper to make a square. Then turn the square into a triangle. What did you do? Explain.

8. **© Assessment** Mark wants to use straws to make a hexagon. Use the dots to draw straight lines that show Mark how the hexagon would look.

© Pearson Education, Inc. 1

Name _____

**Another Look!** You can use different materials to make shapes.

This circle was made with string.

A circle has 0 sides and 0 vertices.

This ⸱r⸱e⸱c⸱t⸱a⸱n⸱g⸱l⸱e⸱ was made with craft sticks.

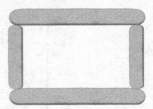

The opposite sides of a ⸱r⸱e⸱c⸱t⸱a⸱n⸱g⸱l⸱e⸱ are equal.

**HOME ACTIVITY** Have your child use materials you have at home to make different shapes. Have him or her count the number of sides for each shape.

Use materials to make each shape. Glue or tape the shape in the box.

1. Make a triangle. Tell 1 thing about a triangle.

2. Make a square. Tell 1 thing about a square.

Draw a picture to solve each problem below.

**3.** Lucia made a shape. The shape has 4 sides. The shape has opposite sides that are equal. What shape did Lucia make?

Lucia made a _____.

**4.** Yani made a shape. The shape has no sides. The shape has no vertices. What shape did Yani make?

Yani made a _____.

**5. Higher Order Thinking** Use shapes to draw a house. Label each shape you used.

**6. © Assessment** Lee made a triangle using toothpicks. He knows that a triangle has 3 sides, but does not know how many vertices it has. Circle each vertex on the triangle below.

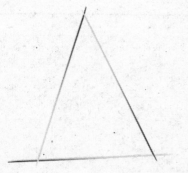

© Pearson Education, Inc. 1

Name _____

**Solve & Share**

Use ⬓ ▱ ▲ to make a ▱.

Show 3 different ways. Write how many of each shape you used in the chart.

**I can ...**
put shapes together to make another shape.

© Content Standard  1.G.A.2
Mathematical Practices  MP.1, MP.4, MP.7

| | ⬓ | ▱ | ▲ |
|---|---|---|---|
| ▱ | | | |
| ▱ | | | |
| ▱ | | | |

| Use smaller shapes to make a larger shape. | Trace the larger shape. | Then use smaller shapes to cover the tracing. | Trace the smaller shapes. |
|---|---|---|---|
|  |  |  |  |

## Do You Understand?

**Show Me!** How can you make a large shape using smaller shapes?

## ☆Guided☆ Practice

Use pattern blocks to make the larger shape.

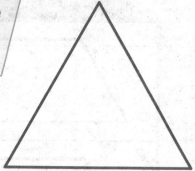

**1.** Complete the chart.

### Ways to Make the Large Triangle

| Shapes I Used | ▱ | ▲ |
|---|---|---|
| Way 1 | 0 | 4 |
| Way 2 | | |

© Pearson Education, Inc. 1

Name _____

**Independent Practice** ☆ Use the smaller shapes to make larger shapes.

**2.** Complete the chart to show a list of ways you can make the hexagon. Use pattern blocks to help.

| Ways to Make | | | |
|---|---|---|---|
| Shapes I Used | | | |
| Way 1 | | | |
| Way 2 | | | |
| Way 3 | | | |

**3.** Use [shapes] to make a [circle].

Draw the [quarter] in the space below.

**4. Higher Order Thinking** Use 3 pattern blocks to make a new shape. Trace the pattern blocks. What shapes did you use? What shape did you make?

_____

_____

**5.** ◎ **MP.1 Make Sense** Two of which shape can make  ?

**6.** ◎ **MP.1 Make Sense** Two of which shape can make  ?

**7. Higher Order Thinking** Name and draw the shape you will make if you put the orange pattern blocks together with their full sides touching. Explain how you know.

_____

_____

_____

**8.** ◎ **Assessment** Nicole wants to make a hexagon.

She has 1  . Which set of shapes could she use to complete the hexagon?

Ⓐ

Ⓑ

Ⓒ

Ⓓ

© Pearson Education, Inc. 1

Name _____

**Another Look!** You can put shapes together to make new shapes.

You can make a

using 3  .

You can make a

using _3_  .

**HOME ACTIVITY** Have your child cut out triangles, squares, and rectangles from old newspapers and magazines. Have him or her use the shapes to make new shapes.

 Circle the shapes you can use to make each shape.

1. Make a  .

2. Make a  .

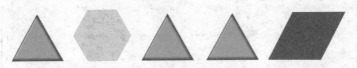

Solve each problem below.

3. **Number Sense** Write the number of each shape needed to make .

_____   _____   _____

4. Kerry uses these shapes to make a new shape.

Circle the shape Kerry makes.

5. Tony uses these shapes to make a new shape.

Circle the shape Tony makes.

6. **Higher Order Thinking** Carlos wants to use 3  to make a square. Can he? Explain.

7. © **Assessment** How many  does Adam need to make a  ?

| I | 2 | 3 | 4 |
|---|---|---|---|
| Ⓐ | Ⓑ | Ⓒ | Ⓓ |

© Pearson Education, Inc. I

Name _____

**Solve & Share**

Use your shapes to make a small boat. Then trace the boat in the space below.

**I can ...**
use shapes to make different shapes.

© **Content Standard** I.G.A.2
**Mathematical Practices** MP.1, MP.2, MP.3, MP.4

You can use shapes to make pictures.

I can use a 🔺 and a 🟩 to make a house!

Add shapes to change the picture.

I can make a larger house! I can add a ▱ and 1 more 🟩.

I can make the house even larger! I can add 2 more 🟩.

Here are more pictures you can make.

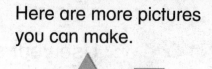

---

**Do You Understand?**

**Show Me!** How do you use shapes to make a picture?

☆ **Guided Practice** ☆ Start with a triangle and use pattern blocks to make a picture. Trace around your shapes to show your picture. Write how many of each shape you used.

I.

© Pearson Education, Inc. 1

## Independent Practice

Use any of the pattern blocks shown to make pictures. Trace around your shapes to show your pictures. Write how many of each shape you used for each picture.

**2.**

---

**3.**

**4.** © **MP.4 Model** Dana started making a flower using these pattern blocks. Draw more leaves and petals to help her finish.

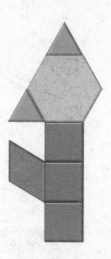

**5. Higher Order Thinking** Use pattern blocks to make a picture of a fish.

**6.** © **Assessment** Jeff is making a model of this arrow. Which shape does he need to add to his model to finish it?

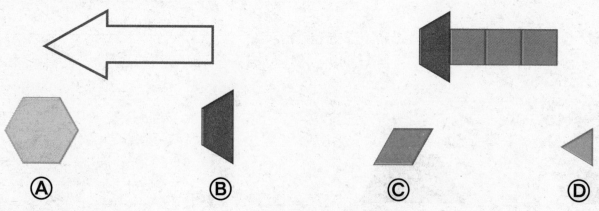

Ⓐ     Ⓑ     Ⓒ     Ⓓ

**Another Look!** You can use different blocks to make the same picture.

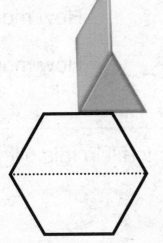

Finish the apple by tracing blocks that make a hexagon without using the hexagon block.

Which shapes did you use? 2 ⬡

Finish the turtle without using triangles.

1.

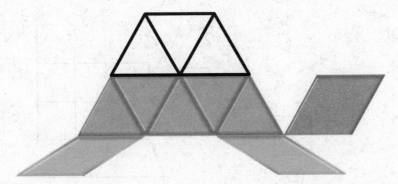

Solve the problems below.

2. © MP.2 Reasoning Write the number of each block used to make this microphone.

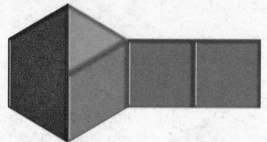

How many triangles? _____     How many squares? _____

How many trapezoids? _____     How many rhombuses? _____

3. **Higher Order Thinking** What are two different ways to fill in this alligator?
Draw or explain how you know.

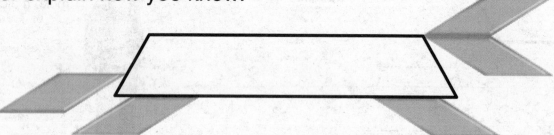

Way 1: _____

Way 2: _____

4. © **Assessment** José is making a picture
of a bunny. He is missing the matching ear.
Which block is missing?

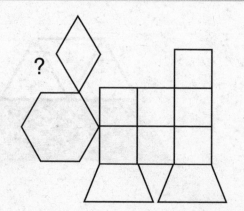

Ⓐ          Ⓑ          Ⓒ          Ⓓ

Name _____

**Solve & Share**

Can you find objects in the classroom that are shaped like the objects below? Write the name of each object you find.

**I can ...**
define 3-D shapes by their number of edges, vertices, and faces or flat surfaces.

© **Content Standard** I.G.A.1
**Mathematical Practices** MP.2, MP.3, MP.8

cube
_____

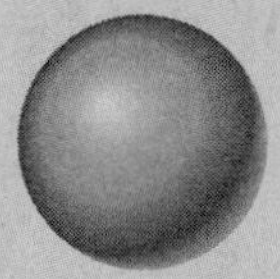

sphere
_____

rectangular prism
_____

cone
_____

cylinder
_____

**Three-dimensional (3-D) shapes** can be grouped in different ways.

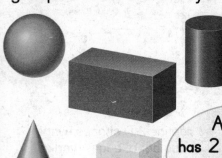

The **flat surface** of each of these shapes is a circle.

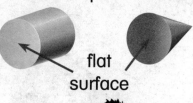

flat surface

*A cylinder has 2 flat surfaces. A cone only has 1.*

These shapes have **edges** and vertices. Their flat surfaces are called **faces**.

edges

vertices

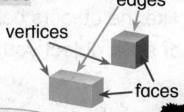

faces

*The faces of the cube and the rectangular prism are all rectangles.*

A sphere is a 3-D shape that has no flat surfaces, no edges, and no vertices.

## Do You Understand?

**Show Me!** Do 3-D shapes always have either faces, flat surfaces, or vertices? Explain.

## ☆ Guided ☆ Practice

Write how many faces or flat surfaces and vertices each 3-D shape has.

| 3-D shape | Number of faces or flat surfaces | Number of vertices | Number of edges |
|---|---|---|---|
| 1.  | 6 | 8 | 12 |
| 2. | | | |

Name _____

## Independent Practice ☆  Write how many faces or flat surfaces and vertices each object has.

| Object | Number of faces or flat surfaces | Number of vertices | Number of edges |
|---|---|---|---|
| 3. | | | |
| 4. | | | |
| 5. | | | |

6. **Higher Order Thinking** Lily has an object that looks like a 3-D shape. The object has 2 flat surfaces and 0 vertices.

Draw an object that Lily could have.

**7.** This shape is a cone. Which shape below is also a cone? How do you know?

_____

_____

_____

**8.** © **MP.2 Reasoning** Nikki and Ben each buy I item from the store. Nikki's item has 4 more edges than vertices. Ben's item has the same number of flat surfaces and edges.

Draw a circle around Nikki's item.
Draw a box around Ben's item.

**9. Higher Order Thinking** Draw and label a 3-D shape. Then write a sentence describing your 3-D shape.

_____

_____

**10.** © **Assessment** I have 6 faces. I have 8 vertices. Which 3-D shape could I be? Choose all that apply.

☐ sphere

☐ cube

☐ rectangular prism

☐ cylinder

Name _____

Help    Tools    Games

**Homework & Practice 14-6**

Use Attributes to Define Three-Dimensional (3-D) Shapes

**Another Look!** Flat surfaces, faces, edges, and vertices can be used to describe 3-D shapes.

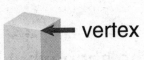

flat surface

 vertex

A cone has 1 flat surface.

A cube has 8 vertices.

A rectangular prism has __6__ faces.

A cylinder has __0__ edges.

**HOME ACTIVITY** Gather household objects that look like the following 3-D shapes: cube, rectangular prism, sphere, cone, and cylinder. Have your child count the number of faces or flat surfaces, edges, and vertices on each shape. Then have him or her choose 2 shapes and tell how they are alike and different.

Circle the 3-D shape that answers each question.

1. Which 3-D shape has 1 flat surface and 1 vertex?

2. Which 3-D shape has 0 flat surfaces and 0 vertices?

Solve the problems below.

**3.** 🔤 **Vocabulary** Circle the number of vertices on a **rectangular prism**.

0 vertices          4 vertices          5 vertices          8 vertices

---

**4.** Circle the shapes that have 6 faces and 12 edges.

**5.** Circle the shape that has 2 flat surfaces and 0 vertices.

---

**6. Higher Order Thinking** Draw or name two 3-D shapes. Find the total number of vertices and faces or flat surfaces.

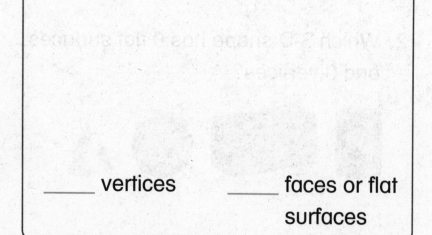

_____ vertices          _____ faces or flat surfaces

**7.** © **Assessment** Katie picks two of these 3-D shapes out of a bag. What is the total number of flat surfaces or faces that could be on the shapes she picked? Choose all that apply.

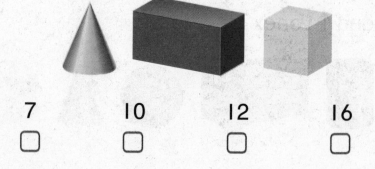

7          10          12          16
☐          ☐          ☐          ☐

**Solve & Share**

Are all three of these shapes considered cylinders? Explain why or why not.

**I can ...**
choose the defining attributes of 3-D shapes.

© **Content Standard** I.G.A.I
**Mathematical Practices** MP.3, MP.7, MP.8

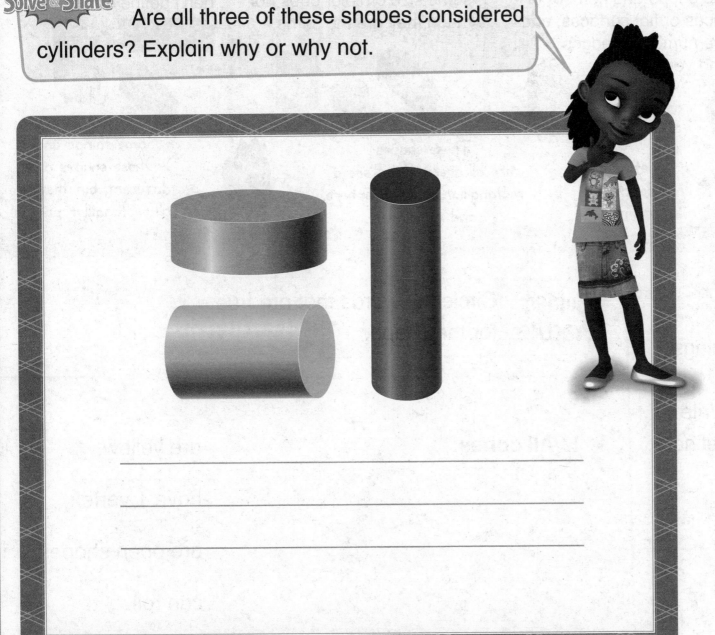

_____

_____

_____

Are these all the same kind of 3-D shape?

We define 3-D shapes by the shape and number of faces or flat surfaces, and the number of edges and vertices.

Just because shapes are the same size or color does not mean they are the same.

Color, size, and direction don't define a shape.

How can I define a rectangular prism?

These shapes are all green. But I see a rectangular prism, a sphere, and a cylinder.

Some things about these shapes are different, but they are all rectangular prisms!

## Do You Understand?

**Show Me!** Write 2 things that are true about all rectangular prisms. Write 2 things that do not define rectangular prisms.

## ☆ Guided Practice ☆

Circle the words that are true for the shape.

1. **All cones:**

are yellow.

( have 1 vertex. )

are open shapes.

can roll.

© Pearson Education, Inc. 1

**Topic 14 | Lesson 7**

Name _____

# Independent Practice    Circle the words that are true for each shape.

**2. All cubes:**

have 12 edges.

have 8 vertices.

cannot roll.

are blue.

---

**3. All cylinders:**

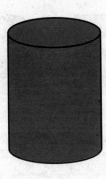

have 2 flat surfaces.

cannot roll.

are red.

can roll.

---

**4. Math and Science** Kevin wants to build a wall. Circle the 3-D shape or shapes he could use to build the wall.

5. © MP.3 **Explain** Do all cubes have the same number of edges?    Yes    No

Explain or draw a picture to show how you know.

6. **Higher Order Thinking** Steve says that both of these shapes are the same because they both have 6 faces and both are purple. Do you agree? Explain.

7. © **Assessment** Match each shape with the words that describe it.

rectangular prism          cube              sphere              cone

6 equal faces              I vertex          8 vertices          no flat surfaces or vertices

Name _____

Help   Tools   Games

**Another Look!** How can you tell if a shape is a cube?

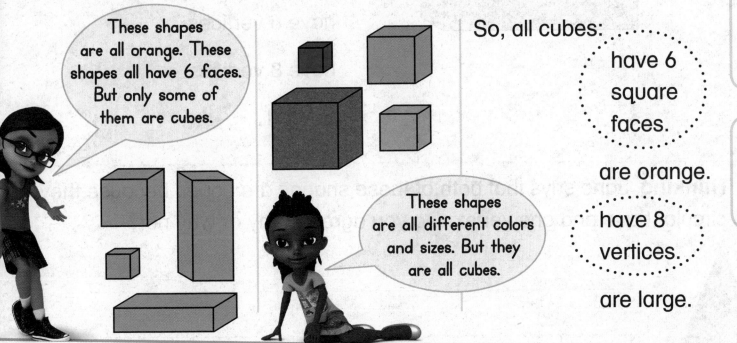

These shapes are all orange. These shapes all have 6 faces. But only some of them are cubes.

These shapes are all different colors and sizes. But they are all cubes.

So, all cubes:

have 6 square faces.

are orange.

have 8 vertices.

are large.

**HOME ACTIVITY** Draw or print out pictures of 3-D shapes and ask your child to tell you one attribute of each shape shown.

Circle the words that are true for the shape.

**I. All spheres:**

have no flat surfaces.

have 3 flat surfaces.

cannot roll.

are blue.

Circle the words that are true for each shape.

2. All rectangular prisms:

have 6 faces.

have 6 vertices.

have 8 vertices.

are red.

---

3. **Higher Order Thinking** Jane says that both of these shapes are cones because they both have one circular base and one vertex. Do you agree? Why or why not?

_____

_____

---

4. © **Assessment** Match each shape with the trait or traits that describe it.

| cone | rectangular prism | cube | cylinder |

| 12 edges | 0 vertices | I vertex | 8 vertices |

Name _____

## Solve & Share

Use green cubes to build a rectangular prism.
Draw and write about the shape you made.

**I can ...**
put 3-D shapes together to make another 3-D shape.

© **Content Standard** 1.G.A.2
**Mathematical Practices** MP.1, MP.2, MP.6, MP.8

**My Drawing**

**About My Shape**

You can combine 3-D shapes to make bigger 3-D shapes.

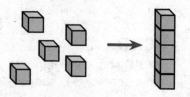

You can build a rectangular prism from cubes.

You can make a big cube from smaller cubes

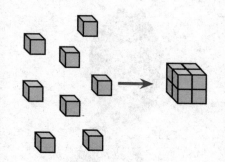

You can also use 3-D shapes to make objects that you know.

What can I make with these?

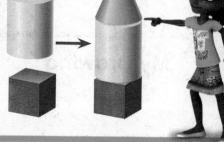

A cube, a cylinder, and a cone make a rocket!

**Do You Understand?**

**Show Me!** How can you find the 3-D shapes that make an object?

**☆Guided Practice☆** Circle the 3-D shapes that could be put together to make the object.

1.   

2.   

**790** seven hundred ninety    © Pearson Education, Inc. 1    **Topic 14** | Lesson 8

**Independent Practice**
Circle the 3-D shapes that could be put together to make the object.

**3.**

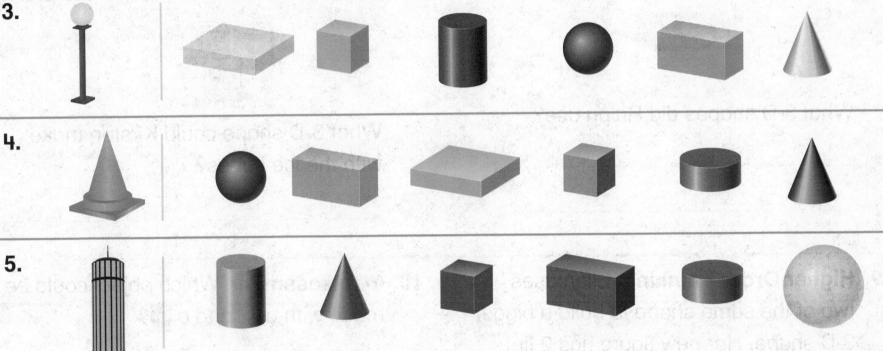

**4.**

**5.**

**6. Higher Order Thinking** Jon wants to combine 6 green cubes to make a bigger cube. Can Jon do this? Explain. Use cubes to help.

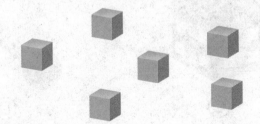

7. © **MP.I Make Sense** Ralph made this shape below with 3-D shapes.

What 3-D shapes did Ralph use?

_____

_____

8. © **MP.I Make Sense** Kirsten has 12 ice cubes. She wants to combine the ice cubes to make an ice sculpture.

What 3-D shape could Kirsten make with the ice cubes?

_____

9. **Higher Order Thinking** Ellen uses two of the same shape to build a bigger 3-D shape. Her new figure has 2 flat surfaces and 0 vertices.

What 2 shapes did Ellen use?

_____

What bigger shape did Ellen build?

_____

10. © **Assessment** Which object could be made with a ▲ and a ▮?

Ⓐ

Ⓑ

Ⓒ

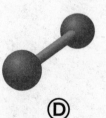

Ⓓ

© Pearson Education, Inc. I
**Topic 14** | Lesson 8

Name _____

**Another Look!** You can combine 3-D shapes to make new shapes.

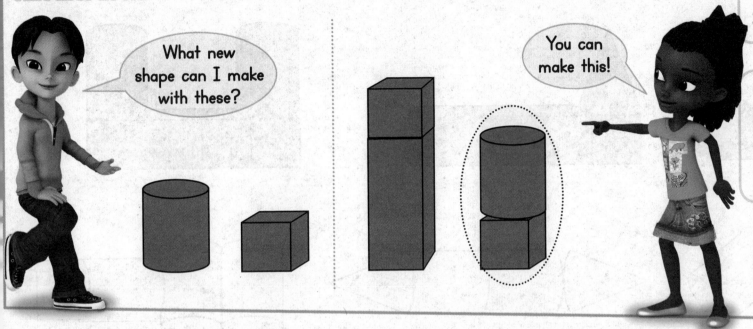

What new shape can I make with these?

You can make this!

**HOME ACTIVITY** Ask your child to show you how to make a new 3-D shape by using household objects such as shoe boxes, soup cans, and funnels.

Look at the two 3-D shapes. Circle the new shape you can make when combining the shapes.

**1.**

**2.**

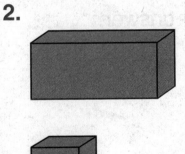

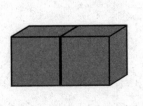 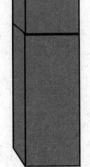

The first two 3-D shapes can be used over and over to make new 3-D shapes. Circle the new shape that could be made by using the first two shapes.

**3.**

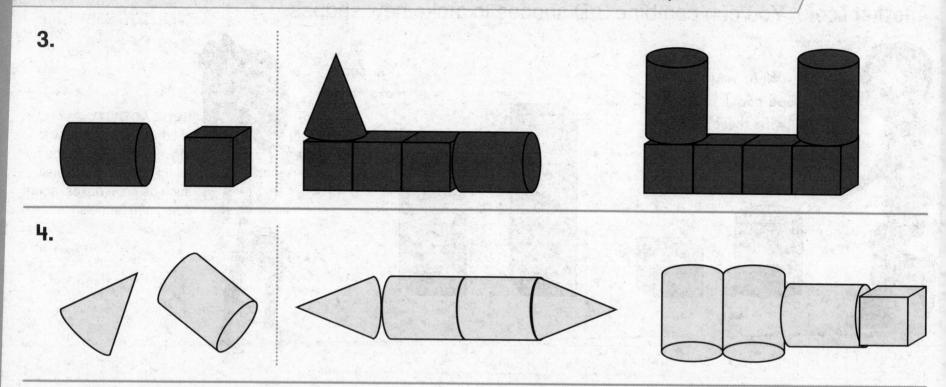

**4.**

5. **Higher Order Thinking** Ramon wants to make a rectangular prism with 5 cubes. Can he do this? Explain. Draw cubes to show your answer.

6. © **Assessment** Which shapes can make a ⬛ ?

Ⓐ
Ⓑ
Ⓒ
Ⓓ

Name _____

Solve & Share

Draw an *X* on all the objects that have flat surfaces that are circles. Tell how you know the flat surfaces are circles. Make sense of the problem by circling the words that are true about the objects you crossed out.

**I can ...**
find the differences in various shapes.

© **Mathematical Practices** MP.I
Also MP.2, MP.6, MP.8
**Content Standards** I.G.A.I,
I.G.A.2

**Thinking Habits**

What am I asked to find?
What else can I try if I get stuck?

| **The objects:** | are white | have 0 edges | have faces |
| | are small | have 0 vertices | have flat surfaces |

All of these shapes are triangles. Circle the words that are true of all triangles.

**How can I make sense of the problem?**

**What's my plan for solving the problem?**

All triangles:
    have 3 sides.
    are blue.
    have a flat bottom.
    are big.
    have 3 vertices.

**I will only circle the words that are true of all triangles.**

All triangles:
    (have 3 sides.)
    are blue.
    have a flat bottom.
    are big.
    (have 3 vertices.)

**I know triangles have 3 sides and 3 vertices.**

**Yes, all triangles have 3 sides and 3 vertices. I have circled the correct words.**

## Do You Understand?

**Show Me!** What words can always be used to describe a rectangular prism?

## ☆ Guided ☆ Practice

Circle the words that are true of the shapes.

1. All of these shapes are squares.

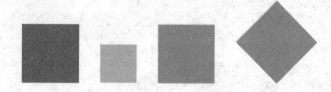

**All squares:**    are orange        are small

                         (have 4 equal sides)    have 4 vertices

© Pearson Education, Inc. 1
**Topic 14 | Lesson 9**

**Independent Practice**

Circle the words that are true of the shapes.
Then explain how you know.

**2.** All of these shapes are cones.

**All cones:**  are blue     have 1 flat surface     have 1 edge     have 1 vertex

_____

_____

**3.** All of these shapes are hexagons.

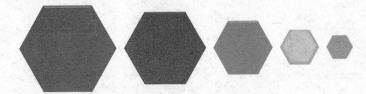

**All hexagons:**  are small     have 6 sides     are blue     have 6 vertices

_____

_____

_____

# Math Practices and Problem Solving

## Performance Assessment

### Arts and Crafts

Wes has cubes, spheres, cylinders, and cones. He wants to use these shapes to make art pieces for an arts and crafts sale at his school.

Wes wants to put together the right shapes for each piece of art.

4. **MP.6 Be Precise** Wes wants to put together one shape that has 6 faces and one shape that has no flat surfaces. What shapes can he use? Explain.

_____

_____

_____

_____

5. **MP.2 Reasoning** Wes puts two cubes together to make a new shape. Tell what shape Wes made and one thing that is true about the new shape.

_____

_____

_____

_____

© Pearson Education, Inc. 1

Name _____

**Another Look!** You can make sense of problems and keep working if you get stuck.

These are rectangles. Circle the words that are true of all rectangles.

**All rectangles:**

(have 4 sides) ⟶ Count the sides. Are there 4?

are blue ⟶ Look above at the rectangles. Are all of the shapes blue?

have 1 long side ⟶ Look at the sides of a rectangle. Is there only 1 long side?

〈have 4 vertices〉 ⟶ Count the vertices. Are there 4?

**HOME ACTIVITY** Have your child gather examples of spheres and cubes (or any other two 2-D or 3-D combination) Ask: "What is true of all spheres (or another 2-D or 3-D shape)?" Help your child identify attributes of each shape he or she finds.

All of these shapes are rectangular prisms. Circle the words that are true of all rectangular prisms.

1. **All rectangular prisms:**

are green          have 12 edges          have 4 faces          have 6 faces

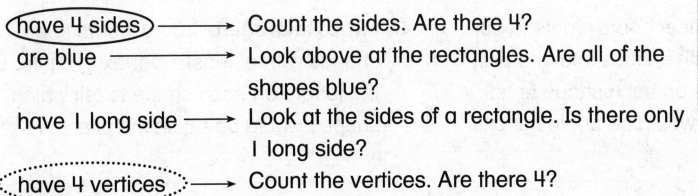

## Puzzle Pieces

Laura is sorting her puzzle pieces into like piles. She has triangles, rectangles, squares, circles, and trapezoids. Help her sort the pieces.

2. **MP.6 Be Precise** Laura wants to put any shapes with 4 sides into one pile. Use the letters on each shape to tell which shapes would be put in the pile.

_____

_____

3. **MP.2 Reasoning** Laura wants to put any shapes with at least 1 vertex in a pile. Use the letters on each shape to tell which shapes would be put in the pile.

_____

_____

4. **MP.1 Make Sense** Sort shapes A–J into two or more piles based on similarities by drawing or writing. Then explain how you sorted.

# Show the Word

Color these sums and differences. Leave the rest white.

| 3 | 2 | 1 |

**I can ...**
add and subtract within 10.

© Content Standard 1.OA.C.6

| 0 + 2 | 5 − 3 | 1 + 1 | 10 − 7 | 1 + 2 | 0 + 3 | 0 + 1 | 10 − 9 | 3 − 2 |
|-------|-------|-------|--------|-------|-------|-------|--------|-------|
| 6 − 4 | 8 − 1 | 8 − 6 | 4 − 1  | 6 + 4 | 8 − 3 | 6 − 5 | 8 + 1  | 5 − 5 |
| 2 + 0 | 2 + 2 | 7 − 5 | 3 + 0  | 2 + 1 | 6 − 3 | 5 − 4 | 9 − 8  | 1 + 0 |
| 4 − 2 | 4 + 3 | 9 − 7 | 9 − 6  | 4 − 4 | 7 + 1 | 2 − 1 | 0 + 8  | 4 + 5 |
| 10 − 8 | 2 − 0 | 3 − 1 | 7 − 4 | 3 + 1 | 2 + 8 | 8 − 7 | 4 + 0  | 8 − 2 |

The word is

_____  _____  _____

# Vocabulary Review

## Word List
- 2-D shapes
- 3-D shapes
- edges
- faces
- flat surfaces
- rectangular prism
- side
- vertex/vertices

## Understand Vocabulary

1. Circle the 2-D shape that has no vertices.

2. Circle the 2-D shape that has 4 vertices and equal sides.

3. Write what part of the shape is shown. Use the Word List.

_____

4. Write the name of the shape. Use the Word List to help you.

_____ prism

## Use Vocabulary in Writing

5. Draw some shapes. Label the shapes using words from the Word List.

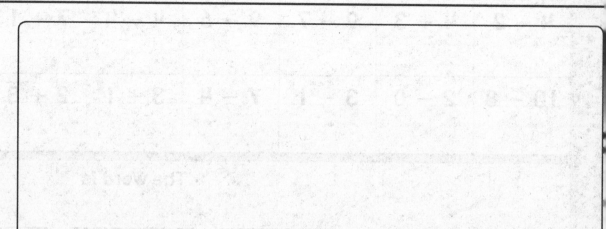

Name _____

## Set A

You can sort 2-D shapes by sides and vertices.

These have sides and vertices.

These have no sides and no vertices.

Solve each problem below.

1. Circle the shape that has 4 straight sides and 4 vertices.

2. Circle the shape that has 0 vertices.

## Set B

You can make 2-D shapes using different kinds of materials.

Construction paper          Toothpicks

Colored sticks          Construction paper

Use materials your teacher gives you to make a rectangle. Glue or tape it in the box.

3.

You can use pattern blocks to make a larger shape.

| |  △ | ⟋ |
|---|---|---|
| Way 1 | 1 | 1 |
| Way 2 | 3 | 0 |

**4.** Make this shape in two different ways.

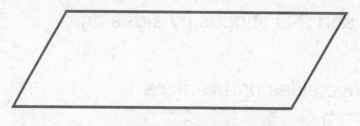

| | △ | ⟋ | ⬟ |
|---|---|---|---|
| Way 1 | | | |
| Way 2 | | | |

You can use pattern blocks to make a picture.

Write the number of blocks you used.

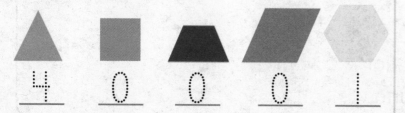

4    0    0    0    1

**5.** Make a picture. Write how many of each block you used.

___    ___    ___    ___    ___

© Pearson Education, Inc. 1

Name _____

## Set E

You can find faces, flat surfaces, edges, and vertices on 3-D shapes or objects.

___6___ faces

___8___ vertices

___12___ edges

___0___ flat surfaces

___0___ vertices

___0___ edges

Write how many flat surfaces, edges, and vertices for each shape.

6.
___ flat surfaces
___ vertices
___ edges

7.
___ flat surface
___ vertex
___ edges

## Set F

You can combine 3-D shapes to make bigger 3-D shapes. Combine 2 cubes.

2 cubes make a rectangular prism.

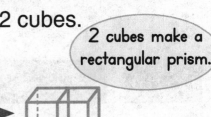

___6___ faces  ___8___ vertices  ___12___ edges

Two shapes were combined to make a new shape. Write the number of flat surfaces, vertices, and edges for the new shape.

8.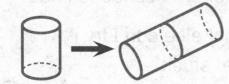

____  ____  ____
flat     vertices  edges
surfaces

All of these are cylinders.

Cylinders are defined by:

___0___ vertices and ___2___ flat surfaces.

Cylinders are **NOT** defined by:

___color___ or ___direction___.

Finish the sentences to define spheres.

9. Spheres are defined by:

_____ and _____.

10. Spheres are **NOT** defined by:

_____ or _____.

**Thinking Habits**

**Persevere**

What am I asked to find?

What else can I try if I get stuck?

Circle the words that are true for all rectangles.

11. **All rectangles:**

have sides of different lengths.

are blue.        have 4 vertices.

© Pearson Education, Inc. 1

Name _____

**1.** Which shape is a square?

Ⓐ ○

Ⓑ △

Ⓒ ▭

Ⓓ ☐

**2.** Which shape has 3 sides?

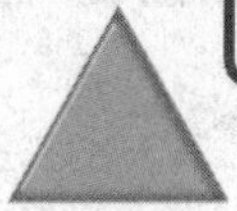

Ⓐ (trapezoid)

Ⓑ (triangle)

Ⓒ (parallelogram)

Ⓓ (square)

**3.** How many flat surfaces and edges does a cone have?

_____ flat surface(s)

_____ edges

**4.** Jaxon makes 3 triangles. Then he puts them together to make a new shape.

Draw a shape that Jaxon could have made.

**5.** Complete the sentence. Then explain how you know you are correct.

 This 3-D shape is a _____.

_____

_____

**6.** Jazmin is making a butterfly. Use pattern blocks to draw in the pieces she is still missing.

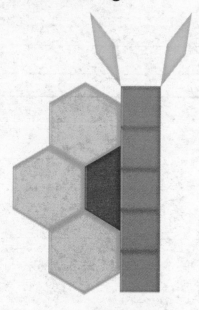

**7.** Which shows the shapes you can use to make ? Choose all that apply.

☐

☐

☐

☐

© Pearson Education, Inc. 1

Name _____

**8.** Which 3-D shape does **NOT** have a vertex?

Ⓐ          Ⓑ          Ⓒ          Ⓓ

**9.** Which 3-D shapes can be used to make this object? Circle all that apply.

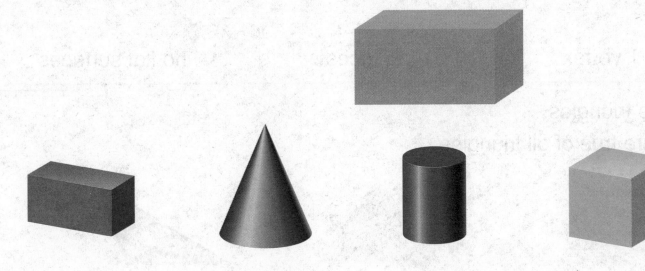

**10.** Which 2-D shape has no straight sides?

 A  B  C D

**11.** Match each 3-D shape with one thing that defines it.

12 edges   I vertex   6 faces   no flat surfaces

**12.** All of these shapes are triangles.
Circle the words that are true of all triangles.

    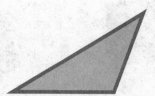

**All triangles:** have 3 sides.  are yellow.

have 3 vertices. are big.

Name _____

## Home Sweet Home!

Leslie uses shapes to make this drawing of her house.

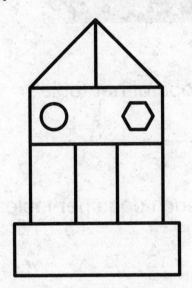

1. Color two of the rectangles in the drawing blue.

2. Explain how you know that the two shapes are rectangles.

_____

_____

3. One of the windows of the house is in the shape of a hexagon.

Show 3 ways you could make a hexagon using smaller shapes. You can use pattern blocks to help you.

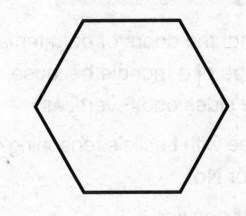

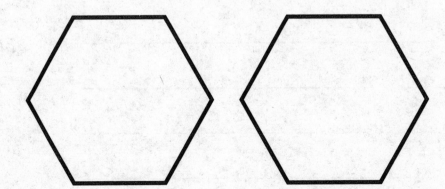

**4.** Leslie has these tents in her backyard.

She says that the doors of both tents are the shape of a triangle because they have 3 sides and 3 vertices.

Do you agree with Leslie's reasoning? Circle **Yes** or **No**.

Explain your answer.

_____

_____

_____

_____

**5.** Leslie has a table in her house that is this shape.

### Part A
What is the shape of her table?

_____

### Part B
How many of each does her table have?

faces _____

edges _____

vertices _____

### Part C
What 3-D shapes could Leslie put together to make her table?

_____

_____

_____

© Pearson Education, Inc. I

# TOPIC 15 Equal Shares of Circles and Rectangles

**Essential Question:** What are some different names for equal shares?

A wheel is a perfect circle.

Wheels help us move people and things much more easily than we could otherwise.

Wow! Let's do this project and learn more.

## Math and Science Project: Wheels and Shapes

**Find Out** Talk to friends and relatives about different objects that have wheels. Ask them how they use wheels in their everyday lives.

**Journal: Make a Book** Show what you found out. In your book, also:

• Draw pictures of different objects that have wheels. Describe the shapes you see. How could you divide the shapes into equal shares?

• Tell how wheels are used to move people or things.

Name _____

# Review What You Know

**A-Z Vocabulary**

**1.** Put an X on the **circle**.

**2.** Draw a **rectangle**.

**3.** Draw the hands on the clock to show a time to the **half hour**.

## Different Kinds of Rectangles

**4.** Color all the rectangles.

Then draw an X on the rectangle that is a square.

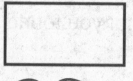

**5.** How many rectangles do you see?

_____ rectangles

## What's the Time?

**6.** Cody gets home at 4:00. He eats a snack a half hour later. Draw the hour and minute hands on the clock to show at what time Cody eats a snack.

# My Word Cards

Study the words on the front of the card. Complete the activity on the back.

A-Z Glossary

## equal shares

There are 2 **equal shares**.

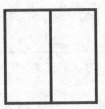

## halves

The circle is divided into **halves**.

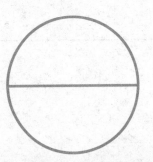

## fourths

The square is divided into **fourths**.

## quarters

The circle is divided into **quarters**, another word for fourths.

# My Word Cards

Use what you know to complete the sentences.
Extend learning by writing your own sentence using each word.

A whole divided into 4 equal shares is divided into

_____,

or quarters.

When a whole is divided into 2 equal shares, the shares are called

_____.

The parts of a whole that are the same size

are _____

_____.

The 4 equal shares of a whole are called fourths or

_____.

Name _____

Draw a line inside the blue circle to show 2 parts that are the same size.

Draw a line inside the yellow circle to show 2 parts that are **NOT** the same size.

**I can ...**
determine if shapes are divided into equal shares.

© **Content Standard** I.G.A.3
**Mathematical Practices** MP.1, MP.4, MP.6, MP.7

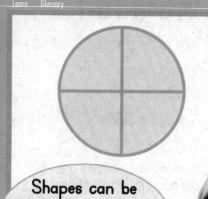

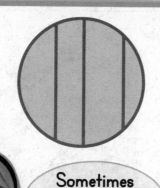

Shapes can be divided into parts, or shares. Sometimes the shares are equal.

Sometimes the shares are not equal.

**Which shows 2 equal shares?**

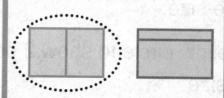

_2_ equal shares

**Which shows 4 equal shares?**

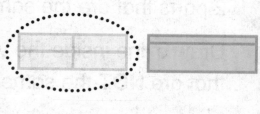

_4_ equal shares

## Do You Understand?

**Show Me!** Is this shape divided into equal shares? Explain how you know.

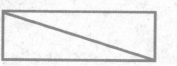

## ☆ Guided ☆ Practice

Decide if each picture shows equal shares. Then circle **Yes** or **No**.

1.

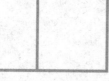

(Yes)   No

2.

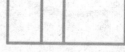

Yes   No

3.

Yes   No

4.

Yes   No

5.

Yes   No

6.

Yes   No

**Topic 15** | Lesson 1

Name _____

**Independent Practice**

Write the number of equal shares in each shape.
If the shares are **NOT** equal, write 0.

7.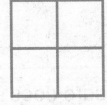

_____ equal shares

8.

_____ equal shares

9.

_____ equal shares

10.

_____ equal shares

11.

_____ equal shares

12.

_____ equal shares

13.

_____ equal shares

14.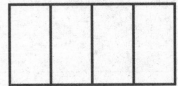

_____ equal shares

15. **Higher Order Thinking** Draw a
square, a circle, or a rectangle.
Divide your shape into equal shares.
Then write the number of equal
shares in your shape.

_____ equal shares

16. © **MP.6 Be Precise** Matt makes a flag with 4 equal shares. Which flag did he make? Circle the correct flag.

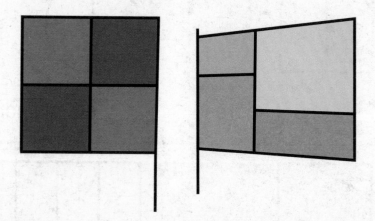

17. © **MP.6 Be Precise** Ruth picks a flag with equal shares. Which flag did she pick? Circle the correct flag.

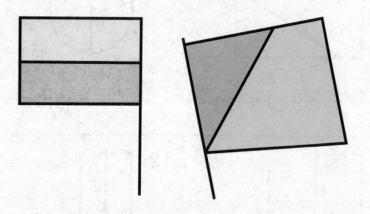

18. **Higher Order Thinking** 4 students share a pizza. Each pizza slice is the same size. Draw a picture of the pizza the students shared.

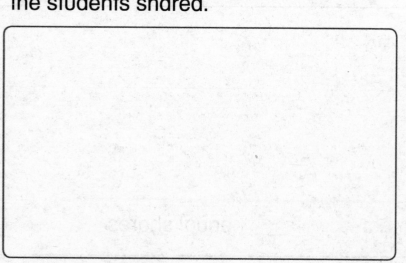

19. © **Assessment** Which square does **NOT** show 4 equal shares?

Ⓐ

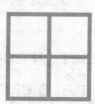

Ⓑ

Ⓒ

Ⓓ

**Topic 15** | Lesson 1

Name _____

**Another Look!** A shape can be divided into shares that are equal or shares that are **NOT** equal.

This rectangle is divided into equal shares.

**HOME ACTIVITY** Draw 2 squares, 2 rectangles, and 2 circles. Have your child divide I square, I rectangle, and I circle into equal shares and I square, I rectangle, and I circle into unequal shares.

This rectangle is **NOT** divided into equal shares.

The shares are the same size.
There are 2 equal shares.

The shares are **NOT** the same size.
There are __0__ equal shares.

Write the number of equal shares in each shape.
If the shares are **NOT** equal, write 0.

I.

_____ equal shares

2.

_____ equal shares

3.
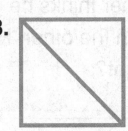

_____ equal shares

Topic 15 | Lesson 1   Digital Resources at PearsonRealize.com   eight hundred twenty-one   **821**

Draw straight lines to divide the shapes into equal shares.

**4.**

2 equal shares

**5.**

4 equal shares

**6.**

2 equal shares

**7. Math and Science** Draw a picture of a bike wheel. Draw lines to divide it into 4 equal shares.

**8. ⓒ MP.6 Be Precise** Has this sandwich been cut into equal shares? Tell how you know.

_____

_____

_____

**9. Higher Order Thinking** Two brothers divide a slice of bread into equal shares. One brother thinks he got a smaller share than the other. How can he check if he is right?

_____

_____

_____

**10. ⓒ Assessment** Which tells how many equal shares the apple has?

Ⓐ 8          Ⓑ 3

Ⓒ 4          Ⓓ 2

Name _____

## Solve & Share

Draw a line inside the circle to show 2 equal shares. Color 1 of the shares. Then write numbers to tell how many shares are colored.

Draw lines inside the rectangle to show 4 equal shares. Color 2 of the shares. Then write numbers to tell how many shares are colored.

**I can ...**
divide shapes into 2 and 4 equal shares and use words to describe those shares.

© **Content Standard** I.G.A.3
**Mathematical Practices** MP.2, MP.3, MP.6, MP.8

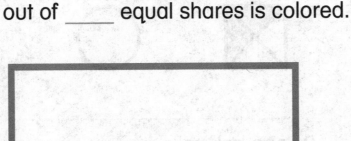

_____ out of _____ equal shares is colored.

_____ out of _____ equal shares are colored.

You can divide shapes into **halves** and **fourths**.

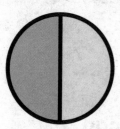

The circle is divided into halves. Half of the circle is yellow.

This rectangle is divided into halves.

2 of the halves make 1 whole rectangle.

This circle is divided into fourths or **quarters**.

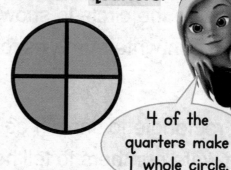

4 of the quarters make 1 whole circle.

One quarter of the circle is blue.

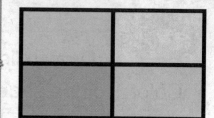

Half of the rectangle is green.
One fourth of the rectangle is yellow.
One quarter of the rectangle is orange.

## Do You Understand?

**Show Me!** What share of the rectangle is green?

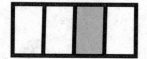

## ☆ Guided Practice ☆

Circle the correct shapes for each problem.

1. one quarter blue

      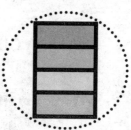   

2. one half yellow

**Topic 15** | Lesson 2

Name _____

## Independent Practice  Color the shapes for each problem.

**3.** one half red

**4.** one fourth orange

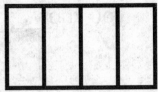

**5.** one quarter green

**6.** one half blue

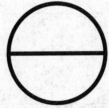

**7. Number Sense** Alex has one half of an oatmeal bar. Jen has one quarter of a different oatmeal bar. Jen's piece is bigger. How could Jen's piece be bigger? Use words or pictures to solve.

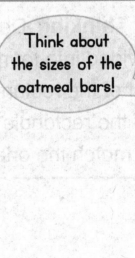

Think about the sizes of the oatmeal bars!

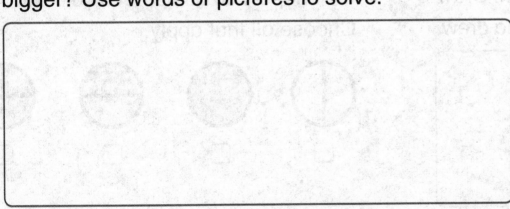

8. © **MP.3 Explain** Sam says the rectangle is divided into halves. Is he correct? Circle **Yes** or **No**. Then explain how you know.

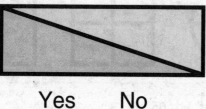

Yes      No

_____

_____

9. © **MP.3 Explain** Mia says the circle is divided into fourths. Lucy says it is divided into quarters. Who is correct? Explain how you know.

_____

_____

10. **Higher Order Thinking** Dana draws a rectangle divided into fourths. She colors one half of the rectangle blue and one quarter of the rectangle green. Draw a rectangle to match the one Dana drew.

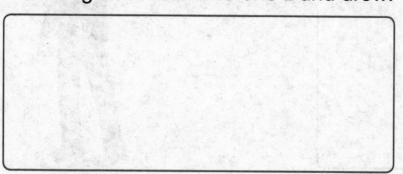

11. © **Assessment** Yao colors a circle. One half of the circle is blue. The other half is **NOT** blue. Which shows the shape Yao could have colored? Choose all that apply.

☐      ☐      ☐      ☐

**Topic 15** | Lesson 2

Name _____

Homework & Practice 15-2
Make Halves and Fourths of Rectangles and Circles

**Another Look!** You can divide shapes into halves and fourths.

Two **halves** make one whole.

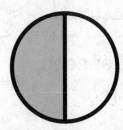

Each share is called a **half**.
One **half** of the circle is green.

Four **fourths** make one whole.

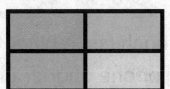

Each share is called a fourth.
One ____fourth____ of the rectangle is green.
One ____quarter____ of the rectangle is blue.

One fourth is the same as one quarter.

HOME ACTIVITY Draw a circle and a rectangle. Have your child divide the circle into two equal shares and color one share. Then have your child divide the rectangle into four equal shares and color one share. Ask: "Which shape shows one half colored? Which shape shows one fourth colored?"

Circle the correct shapes for each problem.

**1. one half blue**

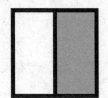

**2. one quarter green**

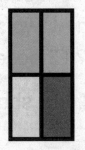

**3. one half yellow**

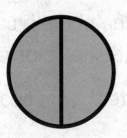 

Topic 15 | Lesson 2      Digital Resources at PearsonRealize.com      eight hundred twenty-seven  **827**

Color the shapes for each problem.

**4.** one half blue

**5.** one quarter purple

**6.** one fourth red

**7. Higher Order Thinking** Color one half of each circle blue. Color one half of each rectangle that is **NOT** a square orange. Color one quarter of each square red.

**8. © Assessment** Sandy divided a rectangle into four equal shares.
She colored one share red, one share blue, and two shares yellow.
How much of the rectangle did she color red? Choose all that apply.

one half                one quarter               two of four shares               one fourth

☐                      ☐                          ☐                              ☐

Name _____

## Lesson 15-3
### Understand Halves and Fourths

Solve & Share

Which is larger: one half or one fourth of the same sandwich?

Divide the sandwiches. Then circle the sandwich that has larger equal shares.

**I can ...**
tell that more equal shares of the same whole creates smaller shares.

© **Content Standard** I.G.A.3
**Mathematical Practices** MP.2, MP.4, MP.5

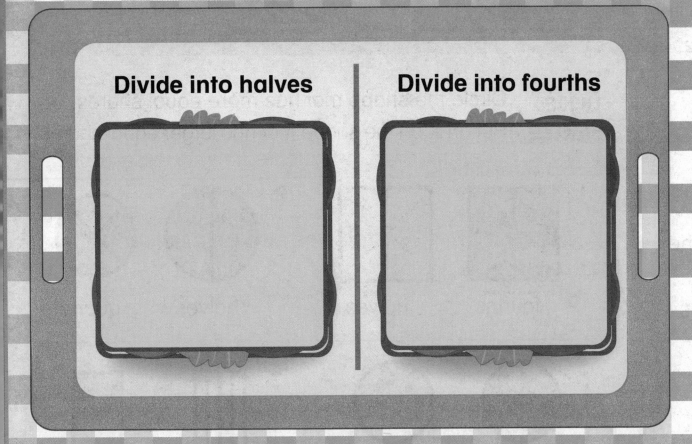

**Divide into halves**        **Divide into fourths**

These pizzas are the same size.

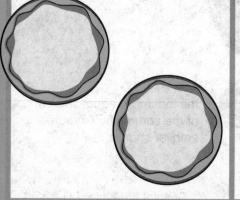

This pizza is cut into 4 equal shares. Each share is one fourth of the whole.

This pizza is cut into 2 equal shares. Each share is one half of the whole.

The pizza with fourths has smaller shares.

The pizza with halves has fewer shares.

| 1 | 2 |
|---|---|
| 4 | 3 |

| 1 | 2 |
|---|---|

## Do You Understand?

**Show Me!** David has a sandwich. Is half of the sandwich more or less food than one fourth of the sandwich? Explain.

## ☆ Guided Practice ☆

Circle the shape that has more equal shares. Put an **X** on the shape that has larger equal shares.

**1.**
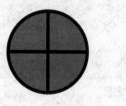
fourths    halves

**2.**
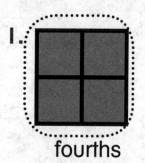
halves    quarters

**3.**

fourths    halves

**4.**
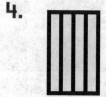 
quarters    halves

© Pearson Education, Inc. 1

**Topic 15** | Lesson 3

Name _____

# Independent Practice ☆  Solve each problem.

**5.** Draw a line to divide this shape in half.

**6.** Shade one quarter of this shape.

**7.** Draw lines in the orange square to make smaller equal shares than are in the blue square.

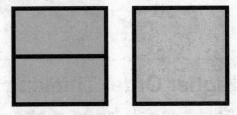

**8. Higher Order Thinking** Joan cuts a rectangle into 2 equal shares. Then she cuts each share in half. How many equal shares are there now? What are these shares called? Use words or pictures to explain.

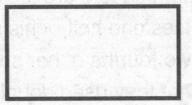

9. © MP.2 Reasoning Steve wants to cut a pan of cornbread into equal shares. Will the shares be larger if he cuts the cornbread into halves or into fourths? Use the picture to help you solve.

The larger shares will be _____.

10. **Higher Order Thinking** Burke and Alisha each have a sheet of paper. Both sheets are the same size. Burke uses one half of his sheet. Alisha uses two fourths of her sheet. Alisha says that they used equal amounts of paper.

Is she correct? Explain your answer. You can draw a picture to help.

11. © **Assessment** Joey has two circles of the same size. He cuts one into halves and the other into fourths. Which words describe how the halves compare to the fourths?

smaller, more      smaller, fewer      larger, more      larger, fewer

Ⓐ           Ⓑ           Ⓒ           Ⓓ

Name _____

Help   Tools   Games

Homework
& Practice 15-3

Understand
Halves and
Fourths

**Another Look!** These rectangles are the same size.
The rectangle with more equal shares has smaller shares.
The rectangle with fewer equal shares has larger shares.

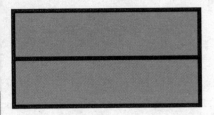

__2__ equal shares
halves
larger equal shares

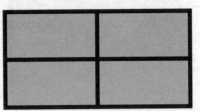

__4__ equal shares
fourths
smaller equal shares

**HOME ACTIVITY** Draw two circles that are the same size. Ask your child to draw lines to divide one circle into halves and one circle into fourths. Then ask your child which circle has more equal shares and which circle has larger equal shares.

Compare the two shapes. Draw lines where you need to. Tell how many equal shares. Then circle **smaller** or **larger** and **more** or **fewer** for each.

1.    quarters

equal shares:

smaller    larger

more    fewer

_____ equal shares

halves

equal shares:

smaller    larger

more    fewer

_____ equal shares

Topic 15 | Lesson 3      Digital Resources at PearsonRealize.com      eight hundred thirty-three **833**

**2.** © **MP.2 Reasoning** Ginny and Martha each have a pizza. Their pizzas are the same size.

Ginny cuts her pizza into fourths. Martha cuts her pizza into halves.

Who has more slices? _____

Who has larger slices? _____

**3.** A-Z **Vocabulary** Divide this square into **halves**. Then shade one half of the square.

**4. Higher Order Thinking** Lucas divides a circle into 2 equal shares. Then he divides each share in half. How many equal shares are there now? What are they called? Use words and pictures to explain.

**5.** © **Assessment** Mary is designing a sign. She wants one half of the sign to be red, one fourth of it to be blue, and one quarter of it to be yellow.

Which shows what Mary's sign might look like?

© Pearson Education, Inc. 1

Name _____

**Solve & Share**

Mary's blanket is divided into 2 equal shares. One share of the blanket is yellow and the other is orange. How can you describe the share of the blanket that is yellow? Complete the sentences below. Then draw and color the blanket to show your work.

**I can ...**
make a drawing or diagram to show a problem about equal shares.

© Mathematical Practices MP.4
Also MP.2, MP.3
Content Standard 1.G.A.3

**Thinking Habits**
Can I use a drawing, diagram, table, graph, or objects to show the problem?

One _____ of the blanket is yellow.

____ of the ____ shares is yellow.

Learn   Glossary

Miss Rose's curtain is divided into 4 equal shares. She dyes 2 shares red and 2 shares blue.

How can you describe the shares of the curtain that are red?

**Can pictures and objects be used to show the problem?**

I can draw a picture of the curtain with 4 equal shares.

You draw a picture to show how the quantities in the problem are related.

I can color in the equal shares to match the problem.

You can use words to describe the drawing.

The drawing shows 4 equal shares. 2 of 4 shares are red.

---

## Do You Understand?

**Show Me!** Amy buys a green and blue rug. It is divided into 4 equal shares. Half of the rug is green. The rest is blue. How many shares are blue? How do you know?

☆ **Guided Practice** ☆  Draw a picture to solve the problem. Then complete the sentence.

1. Pete makes a purple and yellow flag. The flag is divided into fourths. 2 shares are yellow. The rest of the flag is purple. How many of the shares are purple?

   _2_ out of _4_ equal shares are purple.

**836**  eight hundred thirty-six     © Pearson Education, Inc. 1     **Topic 15** | Lesson 4

**Independent Practice** ☆ Draw a picture to solve each problem. Then complete the sentence.

2. Tracy's pizza is cut into halves. She eats 1 of the shares. How many shares of the pizza does she eat?

Tracy eats _____ out of _____ equal shares.

3. Mia cut her sandwich into quarters. 2 of the shares have cheese. What share of the sandwich does **NOT** have cheese?

_____ out of _____ shares do not have cheese.

4. **Algebra** Color the correct number of shares to continue the pattern.

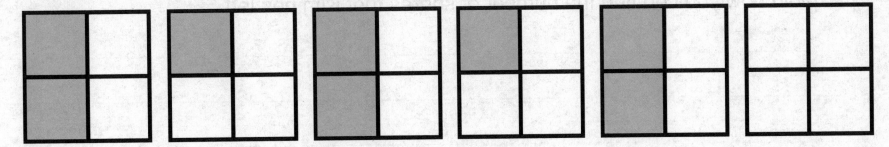

# Math Practices and Problem Solving

## Performance Assessment

**Pizza Shares** Kim cuts a pizza into 4 equal shares. She gives half of the pizza to Stephen.

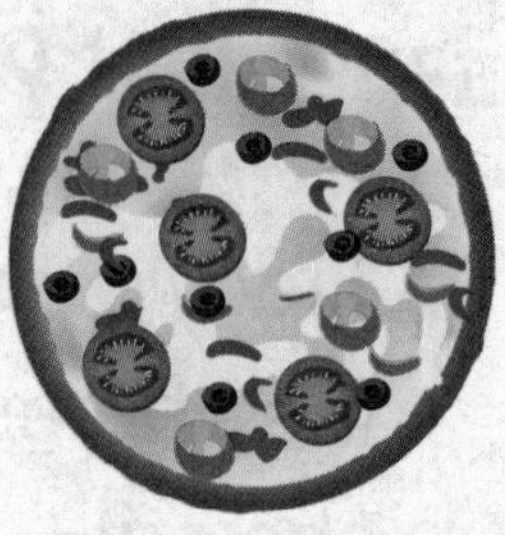

5. **MP.4 Model** Draw a picture to show the shares of the pizza that Stephen has.

6. **MP.2 Reasoning** How many shares of the pizza are left after Kim gives half to Stephen? Write the missing numbers.

_____ out of _____ shares are left.

7. **MP.3 Explain** What if Kim gives Stephen only 1 share of the pizza? Explain how you can find the number of shares that Kim has left.

_______________________________________________

_______________________________________________

_______________________________________________

Name _____

**Another Look!** Dale's flag is divided into 4 equal shares.
2 of the shares are yellow. The rest are green.
How many shares of Dale's flag are green?

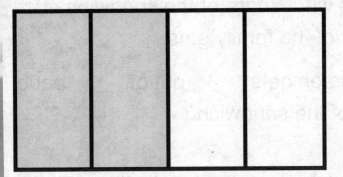

**HOME ACTIVITY** Read this story to your child: "Jack has a mat with four equal shares. Two shares are green. How many shares are not green?" Have your child draw a picture to solve the problem. Ask him or her to solve similar stories. Then write a sentence that goes with each number story.

A picture can help you solve the problem. You can use the math words you know to write a sentence to solve the problem.

The picture can help you see that the shares that are not shaded must be green.

So, __2__ out of 4 shares will be green.

Draw a picture to solve the problem. Then complete the sentences.

1. Sasha's scarf is divided into halves. One of the shares is brown. The rest of the scarf is green.

_____ out of _____ equal shares is brown.

_____ out of _____ equal shares is green.

**Sandwich Shares** The Dawson family buys 1 big sandwich to share equally. There are 4 members of the family.

2. **MP.4 Model** Draw a picture to show how the family members can share the sandwich.

3. **MP.2 Reasoning** Complete the sentence that tells what share of the sandwich each member of the family gets.

   Each person gets _____ out of _____ equal shares of the sandwich.

4. **MP.3 Explain** Rachel is a member of the Dawson family. She gives her share of the sandwich to her brother Gary. What share of the sandwich does Gary have now? Explain how you found the answer using words or pictures.

© Pearson Education, Inc. 1

**Find a Match**

Find a partner. Point to a clue. Read the clue. Look below the clues to find a match. Write the clue letter in the box next to the match. Find a match for every clue.

**I can ...**
add and subtract within 10.

© **Content Standard** 1.OA.C.6

**Clues**

**A** $4 + 2 + 1$

**B** $4 - 1$

**C** $5 - 3$

**D** $2 + 2 + 2$

**E** $5 - 1$

**F** $1 + 3 + 1$

**G** $4 + 4$

**H** $1 + 3 + 6$

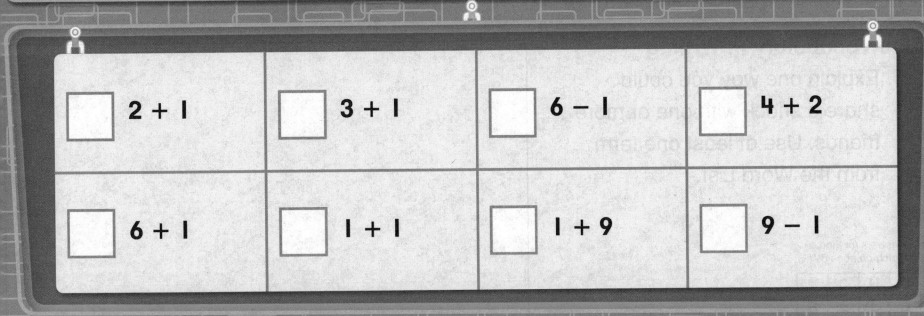

☐ $2 + 1$    ☐ $3 + 1$    ☐ $6 - 1$    ☐ $4 + 2$

☐ $6 + 1$    ☐ $1 + 1$    ☐ $1 + 9$    ☐ $9 - 1$

*Answers for* Find a Match *on next page.*

**A-Z** Glossary

**Word List**
- equal shares
- fourths
- halves
- quarters

## Understand Vocabulary

**1.** Fill in the blank.

I can cut my sandwich into two equal parts called

_____ .

**2.** Fill in the blank.

When you share a sandwich equally with three other people, you cut it into _____ .

**3.** Fill in the blank.

If you want everyone to get the same amount of a sandwich, you need to cut it into _____ .

**4.** Fill in the blank.

Four people share one whole carton of juice and each person gets the same amount. The whole carton is divided into _____ .

## Use Vocabulary in Writing

**5.** Explain one way you could share a snack with one or more friends. Use at least one term from the Word List.

*Answers for* Find a
Match *on page 841*

| G | H | C | A |
|---|---|---|---|
| B | E | F | D |

Name _____

## Set A

You can divide a whole into shares.

4 equal shares

0 equal shares

Write the number of equal shares in each shape. If the shares are **NOT** equal, write 0.

1.

____ equal shares

2.

____ equal shares

## Set B

You can divide shapes into equal shares. You can describe the shares using the words *half* or *fourth*.

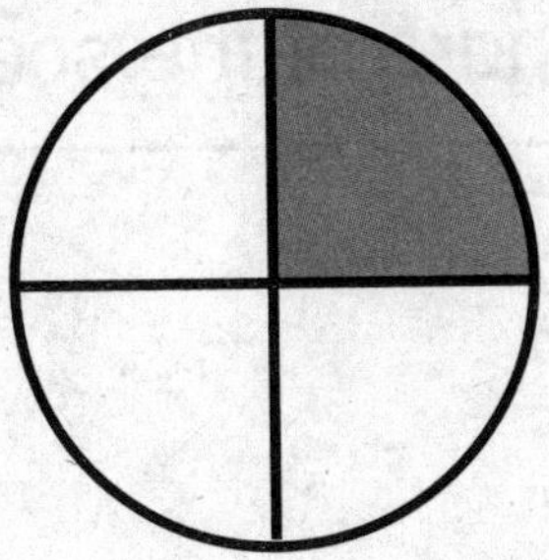

one ___fourth___ blue

Divide and color the shapes for each problem.

3. one half green

4. one fourth orange

You can compare shares of the same shape that are different sizes.

These circles are the same size, but they are divided differently.

The red circle has larger equal shares.

The yellow circle has more equal shares.

Divide the shapes. Then circle the words that complete the sentences.

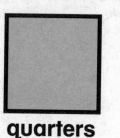 

quarters        halves

5. The blue square has **smaller** / **larger** equal shares than the green square.

6. The green square has **more** / **fewer** equal shares than the blue square.

**Thinking Habits**

**Model with Math**

How can I use math words I know to help solve the problem?

Can I use a drawing, diagram, table, graph, or objects to show the problem?

Draw a picture to solve the problem.

7. Maya's scarf is divided into 4 equal shares. I share is green. 2 shares are yellow. The rest is blue. What share of the scarf is blue?

_____ out of _____ equal shares is blue.

**844**  eight hundred forty-four

Name _____

**1.** Which shape shows 2 equal shares?

Ⓐ          Ⓑ          Ⓒ          Ⓓ

**2.** Which shape does **NOT** show one fourth colored blue?

Ⓐ          Ⓑ          Ⓒ          Ⓓ

**3.** Divide the rectangle into halves. Then color half of the rectangle.
Explain how you know that you colored the right amount.

_____

_____

**4.** Which shape is divided into quarters?

(A)  (B)  (C)  (D)

**5.** Compare the two shapes. Circle the words that describe the equal shares.

quarters     larger equal shares

halves     smaller equal shares

quarters     larger equal shares

halves     smaller equal shares

**6.** Ron draws a flag divided into 4 equal shares. 2 shares are purple and the rest are blue. How many shares of the flag are blue?

Draw a picture to solve the problem. Then complete the sentence.

_____ out of _____ equal shares are blue.

Name _____

**Kerry's Kitchen**

Kerry loves to cook!

She makes many different foods.

1. Kerry bakes a loaf of bread.
   She cuts it into equal shares.
   How many equal shares are there?

_____ equal shares

2. Kerry makes a pizza.
   She cuts it so that she and her sister
   each get an equal share.
   What are the shares called?

   _____

   Show two ways that Kerry could
   divide the pizza.

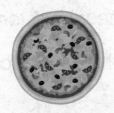 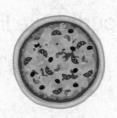

3. Kerry makes a sandwich.
   She eats one half of it.
   Color to show how much
   she ate.

© **Performance Assessment**

How many halves make
the whole sandwich?

_____ halves

Think about what "half" means.

**4.** Kerry makes a pan of oatmeal bars.
She cuts up the bars.
Kerry says that she divided the bars
into fourths.

Is she correct?   Circle **Yes** or **No**.

Explain your answer.

_____

_____

_____

**5.** Kerry makes a salad.
She cuts a tomato into four equal shares.
She puts 1 equal share of the tomato in
the salad.

**Part A**
Draw a picture to show the share of the
tomato that is in the salad.

**Part B**
The equal shares that Kerry cut are
called fourths.
What is another name for these shares?

_____

**Part C**
How many fourths are in the whole tomato?

There are _____ fourths in the whole tomato.

© Pearson Education, Inc. 1

Here's a preview of next year. These lessons help you step up to Grade 2.

# STEP UP to Grade 2

## Lessons

**1** Even and Odd Numbers
**2.OA.C.3, 2.OA.B.2** .............................. 851

**2** Use Arrays to Find Totals
**2.OA.C.4, 2.OA.B.2** .............................. 855

**3** Add on a Hundred Chart
**2.NBT.B.5, 2.NBT.B.9** ........................... 859

**4** Models to Add 2-Digit Numbers
**2.NBT.B.5, 2.NBT.B.9** ........................... 863

**5** Subtract on a Hundred Chart
**2.NBT.B.5, 2.NBT.B.9** ........................... 867

**6** Models to Subtract 2- and 1-Digit
Numbers **2.NBT.B.5, 2.NBT.B.9** ........... 871

**7** Tell Time to Five Minutes **2.MD.C.7,**
**2.NBT.A.2** .............................................. 875

**8** Understand Hundreds **2.NBT.A.1a,**
**2.NBT.A.1b** ............................................. 879

**9** Counting Hundreds, Tens,
and Ones **2.NBT.A.1** ............................ 883

**10** Skip Count by 5, 10, and 100,
to 1,000 **2.NBT.A.2** .............................. 887

Name _____

**Solve & Share**

Use cubes to make the numbers below.
Shade all the numbers that can be shown as two
equal groups of cubes.
What do you notice about the numbers you shaded?

**Lesson 1**

**Even and Odd Numbers**

**I can ...**
tell if a group of objects
is even or odd.

© **Content Standards** 2.OA.C.3,
2.OA.B.2
**Mathematical Practices** MP.4,
MP.5, MP.6, MP.7

| 1 | 2 | 3 | 4 | 5 | 6 | 7 | 8 | 9 | 10 |
|---|---|---|---|---|---|---|---|---|----|
| 11 | 12 | 13 | 14 | 15 | 16 | 17 | 18 | 19 | 20 |

How can you tell if a number is **even** or **odd**?

Use cubes to find out.

8

9

An even number can be shown as two equal parts using cubes.

8 is even.
$4 + 4 = 8$

An odd number cannot be shown as two equal parts using cubes.

9 is odd.
$5 + 4 = 9$

The ones digit tells you if a number is even or odd.

18 is even.
19 is odd.

| 1 | 2 | 3 | 4 | 5 | 6 | 7 | 8 | 9 | 10 |
|---|---|---|---|---|---|---|---|---|----|
| 11 | 12 | 13 | 14 | 15 | 16 | 17 | 18 | 19 | 20 |

## Do You Understand?

**Show Me!** You break apart a tower of cubes to make two equal parts, but there is one cube left over. Is the number of cubes even or odd? Explain.

**☆ Guided Practice ☆** Look at the number. Circle even or odd. Then write the equation.

**1.**

8

odd   (even)

$4 + 4 = 8$

**2.**

11

odd   even

___ + ___ = ___

© Pearson Education, Inc. 1

**Step Up** | Lesson 1

Name _____

**Independent Practice** Look at the number. Circle even or odd. Then write the equation. Use cubes to help.

**3.** 9

odd          even

___ + ___ = ___

**4.** 18

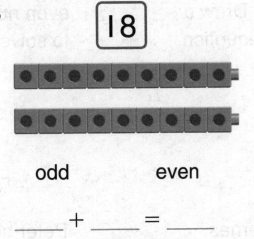

odd          even

___ + ___ = ___

**5.** 10

odd          even

___ + ___ = ___

**6.** 13

odd          even

___ + ___ = ___

**7.** 7

odd          even

___ + ___ = ___

**8.** 6

odd          even

___ + ___ = ___

For each number, circle true or false. Then explain your thinking.

**9. Higher Order Thinking**
Carl says 14 is even.
He says 41 is odd.
True or false?

| 14 | 41 | |
|---|---|---|
| True | True | |
| False | False | |

10. **© MP.4 Model with Math** Lily fills 2 baskets with 7 berries each. She gives both baskets to Ted. Does Ted have an odd or even number of berries? Draw a picture to solve. Then write an equation.

_____ + _____ = _____

Ted has an _____ number of berries.

11. **© MP.4 Model with Math** Peter puts 8 marbles in one jar. He puts 1 marble in another jar. Does Peter have an odd or even number of marbles? Draw a picture to solve. Then write an equation.

_____ + _____ = _____

Peter has an _____ number of marbles.

12. **Higher Order Thinking** If you add two even numbers, will the sum be odd or even? Explain. Use numbers, pictures, or words.

13. **© Assessment** Use the numbers on the cards below. Write two different addition equations. The sum in each equation needs to be an odd number.

_____ + _____ = _____    _____ + _____ = _____

**Step Up** | Lesson 1

Name _____

**Solve & Share**

Show and explain two different ways to find how many circles in all.

**I can ...**
find the total number of objects in a set of rows and columns.

© **Content Standards** 2.OA.C.4, 2.OA.B.2
**Mathematical Practices** MP.1, MP.3, MP.4, MP.7

You can model repeated addition with an array.

Arrays have equal **rows**. Each row has 3 strawberries.

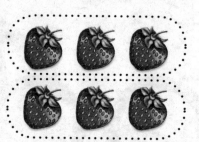

Arrays have equal **columns**. Each column has 2 strawberries.

Write two equations that match the array.

By Rows
$3 + 3 = 6$

By Columns
$2 + 2 + 2 = 6$

## Do You Understand?

**Show Me!** Is this group an array? Explain.

## ☆ Guided ☆ Practice

Write two equations that match each array.

**1.**

By Rows

$\underline{2} + \underline{2} = \underline{4}$

By Columns

$\underline{2} + \underline{2} = \underline{4}$

**2.**

By Rows

$\underline{\phantom{2}} + \underline{\phantom{2}} + \underline{\phantom{2}} = \underline{\phantom{2}}$

By Columns

$\underline{\phantom{2}} + \underline{\phantom{2}} = \underline{\phantom{2}}$

**Step Up** | Lesson 2

**Independent Practice** ✩    Write two equations that match each array.

3.

By Rows _____ + _____ + _____ + _____

=  _____ =  _____

By Columns _____ + _____ + _____ = _____

4.

_____ + _____ = _____

_____ + _____ + _____ + _____ = _____

5.

By Rows _____ + _____ = _____

By Columns _____ + _____ + _____ = _____

6.

_____ + _____ + _____ + _____ + _____ = _____

_____ + _____ + _____ + _____ = _____

7. **Algebra** Use the array to find the missing number.

_____ + 4 = 8

8. © **MP.7 Look for Patterns** Dana places the berries in an array. Write two equations that match the array. How many berries are there in all?

_____

_____

_____ berries

9. The array shows cars in a parking lot. Can you write two different equations that match the array? Explain. How many cars are in the parking lot in all?

_____

_____

_____ cars

10. **Higher Order Thinking** Draw a garden with up to 6 rows that has the same number of plants in each row. Then write two equations that match your array.

11. © **Assessment** Brent sets basketballs in an array. He has 3 rows of basketballs with 4 basketballs in each row. Which equation shows the array Brent made and how many basketballs in all?

Ⓐ $3 + 3 + 3 = 9$

Ⓑ $3 + 3 = 6$

Ⓒ $4 + 4 = 8$

Ⓓ $4 + 4 + 4 = 12$

Name _____

**Solve & Share**

How can you use the hundred chart to help you solve 32 + 43? Explain. Write an addition equation to show the sum.

## Lesson 3
## Add on a Hundred Chart

**I can ...**
add two-digit numbers to two-digit numbers using a hundred chart.

© **Content Standards** 2.NBT.B.5, 2.NBT.B.9
**Mathematical Practices** MP.4, MP.7, MP.8

| 1 | 2 | 3 | 4 | 5 | 6 | 7 | 8 | 9 | 10 |
|---|---|---|---|---|---|---|---|---|---|
| 11 | 12 | 13 | 14 | 15 | 16 | 17 | 18 | 19 | 20 |
| 21 | 22 | 23 | 24 | 25 | 26 | 27 | 28 | 29 | 30 |
| 31 | 32 | 33 | 34 | 35 | 36 | 37 | 38 | 39 | 40 |
| 41 | 42 | 43 | 44 | 45 | 46 | 47 | 48 | 49 | 50 |
| 51 | 52 | 53 | 54 | 55 | 56 | 57 | 58 | 59 | 60 |
| 61 | 62 | 63 | 64 | 65 | 66 | 67 | 68 | 69 | 70 |
| 71 | 72 | 73 | 74 | 75 | 76 | 77 | 78 | 79 | 80 |
| 81 | 82 | 83 | 84 | 85 | 86 | 87 | 88 | 89 | 90 |
| 91 | 92 | 93 | 94 | 95 | 96 | 97 | 98 | 99 | 100 |

_____ + _____ = _____

You can add on a hundred chart.
Find 54 + 18.

Start at 54.
You need to add the tens
from 18. Move down
1 row to show 1 ten.

| 51 | 52 | 53 | 54 | 55 | 56 | 57 | 58 | 59 | 60 |
|----|----|----|----|----|----|----|----|----|----|
| 61 | 62 | 63 | 64 | 65 | 66 | 67 | 68 | 69 | 70 |
| 71 | 72 | 73 | 74 | 75 | 76 | 77 | 78 | 79 | 80 |

Now add the ones.

You're already at 64.
Now move ahead 8 to show
8 ones. You need to go to the
next row to add them all.
So, 54 + 18 = 72.

| 51 | 52 | 53 | 54 | 55 | 56 | 57 | 58 | 59 | 60 |
|----|----|----|----|----|----|----|----|----|----|
| 61 | 62 | 63 | 64 | 65 | 66 | 67 | 68 | 69 | 70 |
| 71 | 72 | 73 | 74 | 75 | 76 | 77 | 78 | 79 | 80 |

## Do You Understand?

**Show Me!** How can you use a hundred chart to add 35 and 24?

## ☆ Guided Practice ☆

Add using the hundred chart.
Draw arrows on the chart if needed.

| 11 | 12 | 13 | 14 | 15 | 16 | 17 | 18 | 19 | 20 |
|----|----|----|----|----|----|----|----|----|----|
| 21 | 22 | 23 | 24 | 25 | 26 | 27 | 28 | 29 | 30 |
| 31 | 32 | 33 | 34 | 35 | 36 | 37 | 38 | 39 | 40 |
| 41 | 42 | 43 | 44 | 45 | 46 | 47 | 48 | 49 | 50 |

1. $14 + 32 = \underline{46}$

2. $22 + 14 = \underline{\phantom{00}}$

3. $\underline{\phantom{00}} = 11 + 20$

4. $16 + 33 = \underline{\phantom{00}}$

**Step Up** | Lesson 3

# Independent Practice    Add using the hundred chart.

| 1 | 2 | 3 | 4 | 5 | 6 | 7 | 8 | 9 | 10 |
|---|---|---|---|---|---|---|---|---|---|
| 11 | 12 | 13 | 14 | 15 | 16 | 17 | 18 | 19 | 20 |
| 21 | 22 | 23 | 24 | 25 | 26 | 27 | 28 | 29 | 30 |
| 31 | 32 | 33 | 34 | 35 | 36 | 37 | 38 | 39 | 40 |
| 41 | 42 | 43 | 44 | 45 | 46 | 47 | 48 | 49 | 50 |
| 51 | 52 | 53 | 54 | 55 | 56 | 57 | 58 | 59 | 60 |
| 61 | 62 | 63 | 64 | 65 | 66 | 67 | 68 | 69 | 70 |
| 71 | 72 | 73 | 74 | 75 | 76 | 77 | 78 | 79 | 80 |
| 81 | 82 | 83 | 84 | 85 | 86 | 87 | 88 | 89 | 90 |
| 91 | 92 | 93 | 94 | 95 | 96 | 97 | 98 | 99 | 100 |

**5.** $23 + 44 =$ _____

**6.** _____ $= 17 + 51$

**7.** $28 + 21 =$ _____

**8.** $16 + 62 =$ _____

**9.** $33 + 38 =$ _____

**10.** $29 + 37 =$ _____

**11.** _____ $= 31 + 17$

**12. Higher Order Thinking** Write the digit that makes each equation true.

$52 + 2\boxed{\phantom{0}} = 75$ | $1\boxed{\phantom{0}} + 81 = 97$ | $38 + \boxed{\phantom{0}}1 = 59$

13. **MP.7 Look for Patterns** Jada has 37 buttons. Mary has 58 buttons. How many buttons do they have in all?

_____ buttons

| 31 | 32 | 33 | 34 | 35 | 36 | 37 | 38 | 39 | 40 |
|----|----|----|----|----|----|----|----|----|----|
| 41 | 42 | 43 | 44 | 45 | 46 | 47 | 48 | 49 | 50 |
| 51 | 52 | 53 | 54 | 55 | 56 | 57 | 58 | 59 | 60 |
| 61 | 62 | 63 | 64 | 65 | 66 | 67 | 68 | 69 | 70 |
| 71 | 72 | 73 | 74 | 75 | 76 | 77 | 78 | 79 | 80 |
| 81 | 82 | 83 | 84 | 85 | 86 | 87 | 88 | 89 | 90 |
| 91 | 92 | 93 | 94 | 95 | 96 | 97 | 98 | 99 | 100 |

14. **MP.7 Look for Patterns** Matt has 40 buttons. Nick has 21 more buttons than Matt. How many buttons does Nick have?

_____ buttons

15. **Higher Order Thinking** 53 plus what number equals 84? Write the steps you take on a hundred chart to find out.

_____

_____

_____

_____

16. **© Assessment** Which weights will balance the weights already on the scale?

Ⓐ

Ⓑ

Ⓒ

Ⓓ

© Pearson Education, Inc. 1

**Step Up** | Lesson 3

Name _____

**Solve & Share**

Leslie collects 36 rocks. Her brother collects 27 rocks. How many rocks do they collect in all? Use cubes to help you solve. Draw your cubes. Tell if you need to regroup.

**I can ...**
use models to add 2 two-digit numbers and then explain my work.

© **Content Standards** 2.NBT.B.5, 2.NBT.B.9
**Mathematical Practices** MP.4, MP.5, MP.6

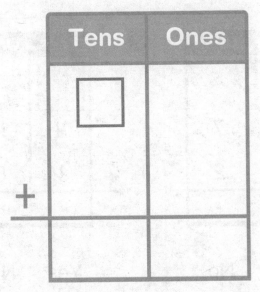

| Tens | Ones |
|------|------|
| ☐ |  |
| + |  |
|  |  |

**Regroup?**

Yes    No

**Let's add!** 37 + 19 = ?

Show 37.
Then show 19.

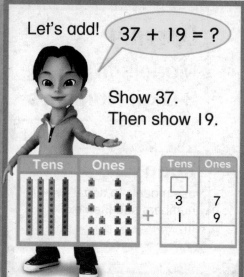

Add the ones.

7 ones + 9 ones = 16 ones

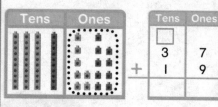

There are 16 ones.
Regroup 16 ones as
1 ten and 6 ones.

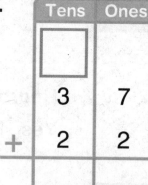

Write **6** ones.
Write **1** to show 1 ten.

Add the tens.

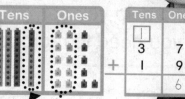

3 tens + 1 ten = 4 tens
4 tens + 1 ten = 5 tens

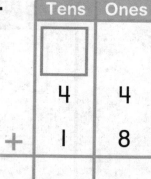

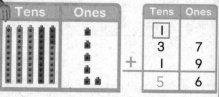

Write **5** to show 5 tens.

---

## Do You Understand?

**Show Me!** When do you have to regroup when adding?

## ☆ Guided Practice ☆

Add. Use connecting cubes and your workmat.
Did you need to regroup? Circle **Yes** or **No**.

**1.**

| Tens | Ones |
|------|------|
|      |      |
| 2    | 9    |
| 2    | 3    |
| 5    | 2    |

(Yes)   No

**2.**

| Tens | Ones |
|------|------|
|      |      |
| 3    | 7    |
| 2    | 2    |
|      |      |

Yes   No

**3.**

| Tens | Ones |
|------|------|
|      |      |
| 4    | 4    |
| 1    | 8    |
|      |      |

Yes   No

---

© Pearson Education, Inc. 1

**Step Up** | Lesson 4

# Independent Practice   Add. Use connecting cubes and your workmat.

**4.**

| Tens | Ones |
|------|------|
|      |      |
| 2    | 7    |
| + 5  | 5    |
|      |      |

**5.**

| Tens | Ones |
|------|------|
|      |      |
| 1    | 9    |
| + 3  | 2    |
|      |      |

**6.**

| Tens | Ones |
|------|------|
|      |      |
| 4    | 3    |
| + 1  | 7    |
|      |      |

**7.**

| Tens | Ones |
|------|------|
|      |      |
| 1    | 4    |
| + 2  | 1    |
|      |      |

**8.**

| Tens | Ones |
|------|------|
|      |      |
| 3    | 1    |
| + 4  | 9    |
|      |      |

**9.**

| Tens | Ones |
|------|------|
|      |      |
| 5    | 6    |
| + 3  | 3    |
|      |      |

**10.**

| Tens | Ones |
|------|------|
|      |      |
| 5    | 7    |
| + 1  | 5    |
|      |      |

**11.**

| Tens | Ones |
|------|------|
|      |      |
| 6    | 5    |
| + 1  | 6    |
|      |      |

**12.**

| Tens | Ones |
|------|------|
|      |      |
| 3    | 9    |
| + 1  | 8    |
|      |      |

**13.**

| Tens | Ones |
|------|------|
|      |      |
| 1    | 2    |
| + 5  | 6    |
|      |      |

**14. Higher Order Thinking** Draw the second addend.

First Addend          Second Addend               Sum

     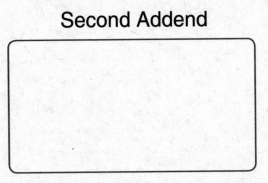     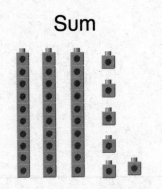

# Math Practices and Problem Solving    Solve the problems below.

**15. © MP.5 Use Tools** Trent builds a fort with 28 blocks. Ryan uses 26 blocks to make it bigger. How many blocks are used in all?

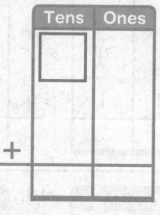

_____ blocks

**16. © MP.5 Use Tools** Greg counts 32 buttons. Then he counts 30 more. How many buttons does Greg count in all?

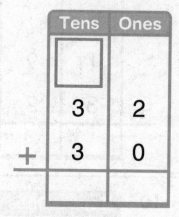

_____ buttons

**17. Higher Order Thinking** Write an addition story about the notebooks and pencils in your classroom. Use pictures, numbers, or words.

**18. © Assessment** Maria has 33 pennies. Her mom gives her 19 pennies and 7 nickels. How many pennies does Maria have now?

Ⓐ 41

Ⓑ 49

Ⓒ 51

Ⓓ 52

© Pearson Education, Inc. 1

**Solve & Share**

How can you use the hundred chart to help you solve 57 − 23? Explain. Write a subtraction equation.

| 1 | 2 | 3 | 4 | 5 | 6 | 7 | 8 | 9 | 10 |
|---|---|---|---|---|---|---|---|---|---|
| 11 | 12 | 13 | 14 | 15 | 16 | 17 | 18 | 19 | 20 |
| 21 | 22 | 23 | 24 | 25 | 26 | 27 | 28 | 29 | 30 |
| 31 | 32 | 33 | 34 | 35 | 36 | 37 | 38 | 39 | 40 |
| 41 | 42 | 43 | 44 | 45 | 46 | 47 | 48 | 49 | 50 |
| 51 | 52 | 53 | 54 | 55 | 56 | 57 | 58 | 59 | 60 |
| 61 | 62 | 63 | 64 | 65 | 66 | 67 | 68 | 69 | 70 |
| 71 | 72 | 73 | 74 | 75 | 76 | 77 | 78 | 79 | 80 |
| 81 | 82 | 83 | 84 | 85 | 86 | 87 | 88 | 89 | 90 |
| 91 | 92 | 93 | 94 | 95 | 96 | 97 | 98 | 99 | 100 |

**I can ...**

subtract two-digit numbers from two-digit numbers using a hundred chart.

 **Content Standards** 2.NBT.B.5, 2.NBT.B.9
**Mathematical Practices** MP.2, MP.4, MP.7, MP.8

____ − ____ = ____

Find 43 − 28 using a hundred chart.

**I need to find the difference between 28 and 43.**

Start at 28. Count to the next number that matches the ones in 43.

| 21 | 22 | 23 | 24 | 25 | 26 | 27 | 28 | 29 | 30 |
|----|----|----|----|----|----|----|----|----|----|
| 31 | 32 | 33 | 34 | 35 | 36 | 37 | 38 | 39 | 40 |
| 41 | 42 | 43 | 44 | 45 | 46 | 47 | 48 | 49 | 50 |

**Count by ones! I counted 5 ones to get from 28 to 33.**

Count by tens to 43.

| 21 | 22 | 23 | 24 | 25 | 26 | 27 | 28 | 29 | 30 |
|----|----|----|----|----|----|----|----|----|----|
| 31 | 32 | 33 | 34 | 35 | 36 | 37 | 38 | 39 | 40 |
| 41 | 42 | 43 | 44 | 45 | 46 | 47 | 48 | 49 | 50 |

**That's 1 ten, or 10 more.**

**I added 5 and 10. That makes 15.**

28 + 15 = 43
So, 43 − 28 = 15.

## Do You Understand?

**Show Me!** How can you use a hundred chart to find the difference between 18 and 60?

## ☆ Guided Practice ☆

Subtract using the hundred chart. Draw arrows if you need to.

| 21 | 22 | 23 | 24 | 25 | 26 | 27 | 28 | 29 | 30 |
|----|----|----|----|----|----|----|----|----|----|
| 31 | 32 | 33 | 34 | 35 | 36 | 37 | 38 | 39 | 40 |
| 41 | 42 | 43 | 44 | 45 | 46 | 47 | 48 | 49 | 50 |
| 51 | 52 | 53 | 54 | 55 | 56 | 57 | 58 | 59 | 60 |
| 61 | 62 | 63 | 64 | 65 | 66 | 67 | 68 | 69 | 70 |

I. 58 − 24 = __34__

2. 41 − 21 = _____

3. _____ = 53 − 32

4. 64 − 23 = _____

## Independent Practice ☆  Subtract using the hundred chart. Draw arrows if you need to.

| 1 | 2 | 3 | 4 | 5 | 6 | 7 | 8 | 9 | 10 |
|---|---|---|---|---|---|---|---|---|---|
| 11 | 12 | 13 | 14 | 15 | 16 | 17 | 18 | 19 | 20 |
| 21 | 22 | 23 | 24 | 25 | 26 | 27 | 28 | 29 | 30 |
| 31 | 32 | 33 | 34 | 35 | 36 | 37 | 38 | 39 | 40 |
| 41 | 42 | 43 | 44 | 45 | 46 | 47 | 48 | 49 | 50 |
| 51 | 52 | 53 | 54 | 55 | 56 | 57 | 58 | 59 | 60 |
| 61 | 62 | 63 | 64 | 65 | 66 | 67 | 68 | 69 | 70 |
| 71 | 72 | 73 | 74 | 75 | 76 | 77 | 78 | 79 | 80 |
| 81 | 82 | 83 | 84 | 85 | 86 | 87 | 88 | 89 | 90 |
| 91 | 92 | 93 | 94 | 95 | 96 | 97 | 98 | 99 | 100 |

**5.** $86 - 34 =$ _____

**6.** _____ $= 77 - 42$

**7.** $55 - 22 =$ _____

**8.** $88 - 51 =$ _____

**9.** $73 - 21 =$ _____

**10.** _____ $= 98 - 56$

**11.** $82 - 61 =$ _____

**12. Higher Order Thinking** Write the digit that makes each equation true.

$57 - \boxed{\phantom{0}}2 = 15$

$7\boxed{\phantom{0}} - 36 = 42$

$48 - \boxed{\phantom{0}}1 = 17$

$98 - 37 = \boxed{\phantom{0}}1$

$56 - \boxed{\phantom{0}}2 = 34$

$89 - \boxed{\phantom{0}}3 = 26$

13. Enrico's puzzle has 75 pieces.
Enrico fits 53 pieces together.
How many more pieces does Enrico still
need to fit together to complete the puzzle?

_____ − _____ = _____

_____ pieces

| 41 | 42 | 43 | 44 | 45 | 46 | 47 | 48 | 49 | 50 |
|----|----|----|----|----|----|----|----|----|-----|
| 51 | 52 | 53 | 54 | 55 | 56 | 57 | 58 | 59 | 60 |
| 61 | 62 | 63 | 64 | 65 | 66 | 67 | 68 | 69 | 70 |
| 71 | 72 | 73 | 74 | 75 | 76 | 77 | 78 | 79 | 80 |
| 81 | 82 | 83 | 84 | 85 | 86 | 87 | 88 | 89 | 90 |
| 91 | 92 | 93 | 94 | 95 | 96 | 97 | 98 | 99 | 100 |

14. © MP.2 Reasoning A book has 65 pages.
Gloria needs to read 22 more
pages to finish the book.
How many pages has
Gloria read already? _____

15. **Higher Order Thinking** Felix wants to
subtract 89 − 47. Write the steps Felix
can take to subtract 47 from 89 on the
hundred chart.

_____

_____

_____

16. © **Assessment** Lee has 98 marbles.
23 of the marbles are blue.
14 marbles are green.
The rest of the marbles are red.
How many marbles are red?

Ⓐ 37

Ⓑ 61

Ⓒ 75

Ⓓ 84

Name _____

**Solve & Share**

There are 22 students drawing pictures.
4 of them finish drawing. How many students are still drawing?
Use cubes to help you solve. Show the tens and ones you have.

| Tens | Ones |
|------|------|
|      |      |

**I can ...**
use a model to subtract a 1-digit number from a 2-digit number.

© **Content Standards** 2.NBT.B.5, 2.NBT.B.9
**Mathematical Practices** MP.2, MP.3, MP.4, MP.5

_____ tens          _____ ones

22 − 4 = _____

Find 32 − 5.

There are not enough ones to subtract.

| Tens | Ones |
|------|------|
| ||| | ⋮⋮ |

− 

| Tens | Ones |
|------|------|
| 3 | 2 |
|   | 5 |

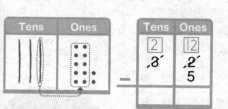

Regroup 1 ten as 10 ones.

Write 2 to show 2 tens.
Write 12 to show 12 ones.

| Tens | Ones |
|------|------|
| |||| | ⋮⋮⋮ |

− 

| Tens | Ones |
|------|------|
| 2 3̸ | 12 2̸ |
|   | 5 |

Subtract the ones.
Then subtract the tens.

| Tens | Ones |
|------|------|
| || | ⋮⋮ ✗✗✗✗ |

− 

| Tens | Ones |
|------|------|
| 2 3̸ | 12 2̸ |
|   | 5 |
| 2 | 7 |

There are 2 tens and 7 ones left.

So,
32 − 5 = __27__.

| Tens | Ones |
|------|------|
| || | ⋮⋮ |

− 

| Tens | Ones |
|------|------|
| 2 3̸ | 12 2̸ |
|   | 5 |
| 2 | 7 |

---

## Do You Understand?

**Show Me!** Why do you need to regroup when you subtract 32 − 5?

## ☆ Guided Practice ☆

Subtract. Draw place-value blocks to show your work. Regroup if you need to.

**1.**

| Tens | Ones |
|------|------|
| 3 | 13 |
| 4̸ | 3̸ |
|   | 6 |
| 3 | 7 |

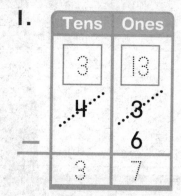

**2.**

| Tens | Ones |
|------|------|
|  |  |
| 2 | 5 |
|   | 8 |

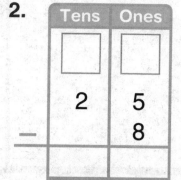

| Tens | Ones |
|------|------|
|  |  |

**Step Up** | Lesson 6

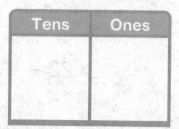
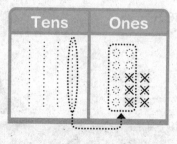

Tools   Assessment

## Independent ⭐ Practice

Subtract. Draw place-value blocks to show your work. Regroup if you need to.

**3.**

| Tens | Ones |
|------|------|
| ☐ | ☐ |
| 3 | 3 |
| − | 3 |

| Tens | Ones |
|------|------|
| | |

**4.**

| Tens | Ones |
|------|------|
| ☐ | ☐ |
| 9 | 1 |
| − | 4 |

| Tens | Ones |
|------|------|
| | |

**5.**

| Tens | Ones |
|------|------|
| ☐ | ☐ |
| 6 | 1 |
| − | 9 |

| Tens | Ones |
|------|------|
| | |

Write the missing number in the box.

**6. Higher Order Thinking** What numbers will complete the subtraction equations?

$$\boxed{\phantom{0}} - 9 = 17$$

$$43 - \boxed{\phantom{0}} = 37$$

# Math Practices and Problem Solving   Solve the problems below.

**7.** © **MP.2 Reasoning** There are 14 students playing with blocks. 9 students go home. How many students are still playing with blocks?

| Tens | Ones |
|------|------|
|      |      |
|      |      |

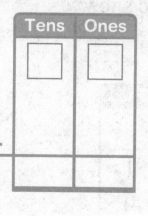

_____ students

**8.** © **MP.2 Reasoning** There are 13 books on the shelf. Amy takes 2 of them. How many books are left on the shelf?

| Tens | Ones |
|------|------|
|      |      |
|      |      |

_____ books

**9.** **Higher Order Thinking** What mistake did Monica make when she subtracted 24 − 4? Show how to fix her mistake.

```
   24
 −  4
 ────
   10
```

| Tens | Ones |
|------|------|
|      |      |
|      |      |

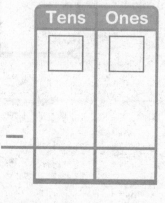

**10.** © **Assessment** Liesel collected 36 leaves. She put some of them in a book. She had 9 leaves left. How many leaves did she put in the book?

Ⓐ 27

Ⓑ 37

Ⓒ 28

Ⓓ 45

_____

_____

_____

_____

Name _____

**Solve & Share**

An airplane is due to arrive at 3:15.
How can you show this time on the clock below? Explain.

## Lesson 7
**Tell Time to
Five Minutes**

**I can ...**
tell time to the nearest
5 minutes.

© **Content Standards** 2.MD.C.7,
2.NBT.A.2
**Mathematical Practices** MP.2,
MP.5, MP.6, MP.8

## Both clocks show 8:05.

The minute hand moves from number to number in 5 minutes.

To tell time to five minutes, count by 5s. Both clocks show 8:35.

I can start at 8:00 and count by 5s to tell the time.

There are 60 minutes in I hour.

The minutes start over again each hour.

## Do You Understand?

**Show Me!** The time is 9:35. What time will it be in 5 minutes?

In I5 minutes?

In 25 minutes?

☆**Guided**☆ Complete the clocks so both
**Practice** clocks show the same time.

I.

2.

3.

4.

© Pearson Education, Inc. I

Name _____

# Independent Practice

Complete the clocks so both clocks show the same time.

**5.**

**6.**

**7.**

**8.**

**9.**

**10.**

**11. Number Sense** Complete the pattern.

**Step Up** | Lesson 7

**12. © MP.8 Generalize** What time is 15 minutes past the time on the green clock and 15 minutes before the time on the orange clock?

_____

**13. Number Sense** Look at the time on the first clock.
What time was it 5 minutes ago?
Write that time on the second clock.

**14. Higher Order Thinking** Draw a clock that shows the time you wake up in the morning. Explain how you know you showed the correct time.

_____

_____

_____

**15. © Assessment** The minute hand is pointing to the 10. Which number will it be pointing to 10 minutes later?

Ⓐ 12

Ⓑ 11

Ⓒ 10

Ⓓ 9

© Pearson Education, Inc. 1

Name _____

What is another way to show 100?
Draw a picture and explain.

**I can ...**
understand place value and
count by hundreds to 1,000.

© **Content Standards** 2.NBT.A.1a,
2.NBT.A.1b
**Mathematical Practices** MP.2,
MP.4, MP.5, MP.7

**Way 1**

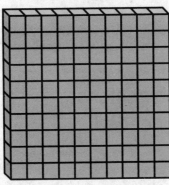

**Way 2**

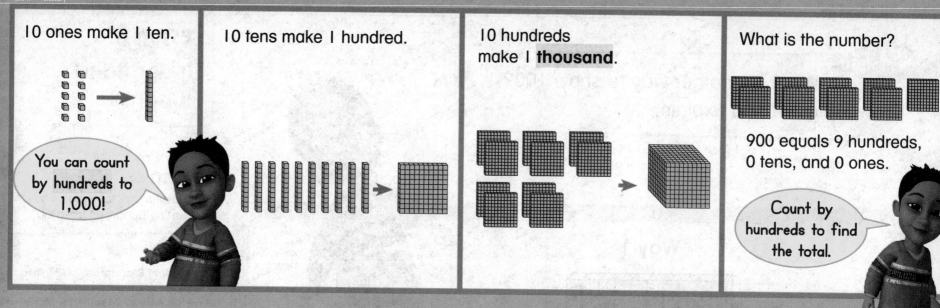

10 ones make 1 ten.

You can count by hundreds to 1,000!

10 tens make 1 hundred.

10 hundreds make 1 **thousand**.

What is the number?

900 equals 9 hundreds, 0 tens, and 0 ones.

Count by hundreds to find the total.

## Do You Understand?

**Show Me!** 10 ones make 1 ten. 10 tens make 1 hundred. 10 hundreds make 1 thousand. Do you see a pattern? Explain.

## ☆ Guided ☆ Practice

Complete each sentence. Use models if needed.

1.  _300_ equals _3_ hundreds, _0_ tens, and _0_ ones.

2.  _____ equals _____ hundreds, _____ tens, and _____ ones.

**880**  eight hundred eighty

**Step Up** | Lesson 8

Tools  Assessment

# Independent Practice  Complete each sentence. Use models if needed.

3. 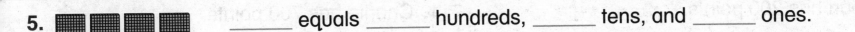 _____ equals _____ hundreds, _____ tens, and _____ ones.

4. _____ equals _____ hundreds, _____ tens, and _____ ones.

5. _____ equals _____ hundreds, _____ tens, and _____ ones.

6. _____ equals _____ hundreds, _____ tens, and _____ ones.

7. **Number Sense** Complete the pattern.

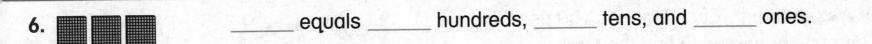

| 1,000 | 900 | 800 | | 600 | | 400 | 300 | 200 | |
|---|---|---|---|---|---|---|---|---|---|

8. © **MP.5 Use Tools** Patti picked a number. She says her number has 2 hundreds, 0 tens, and 0 ones.

What is Patti's number?

_____

9. A-Z **Vocabulary** Complete the sentences using the words below.

**hundred      tens      ones**

There are 10 _____ in one hundred.

There are 100 _____ in one _____.

**Higher Order Thinking** Pearl and Charlie are playing beanbag toss. Circle the two numbers they each must get to score 1,000.

10. Pearl has 200 points.

200      500      600      100

11. Charlie has 700 points.

100      200      400      700

12. © **Assessment** Each box has 100 pencils. Count by hundreds to find the total. Which number tells how many pencils are in the boxes?

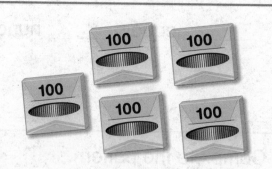

Ⓐ 700

Ⓑ 550

Ⓒ 500

Ⓓ 150

Name _____

**Solve & Share**

How can you use place-value blocks to show 125? Explain.

**Lesson 9**
Counting Hundreds, Tens, and Ones

**I can ...**
count different types of place-value blocks to determine the number being shown.

 **Content Standard** 2.NBT.A.1
**Mathematical Practices** MP.2, MP.4, MP.7

What number do the models show?

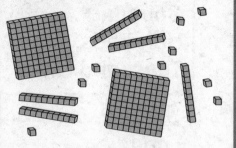

Remember, 10 ones make 1 ten.
10 tens make 1 **hundred**.

First, count the hundreds.

| Hundreds | Tens | Ones |
|----------|------|------|
| 2 | | |

Then count the tens.

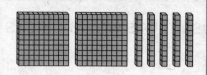

| Hundreds | Tens | Ones |
|----------|------|------|
| 2 | 5 | |

Then count the ones.

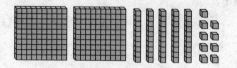

| Hundreds | Tens | Ones |
|----------|------|------|
| 2 | 5 | 9 |

The models show 259. 259 has 3 digits.

## Do You Understand?

**Show Me!** How many hundreds are in 395? How many tens? How many ones?

## ☆Guided Practice☆

Write the numbers shown.
Use models and your workmat if needed.

1.

| Hundreds | Tens | Ones |
|----------|------|------|
| | 7 | 7 |

77

2.

| Hundreds | Tens | Ones |
|----------|------|------|
| | | |

_____

© Pearson Education, Inc. 1

Tools  Assessment

## Independent Practice

Write the numbers shown. Use models and your workmat if needed.

3.

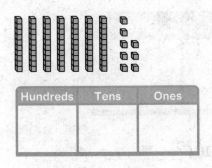

| Hundreds | Tens | Ones |
|----------|------|------|
|          |      |      |

_____

4.

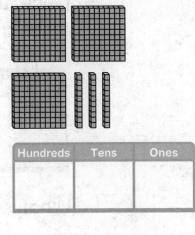

| Hundreds | Tens | Ones |
|----------|------|------|
|          |      |      |

_____

5.

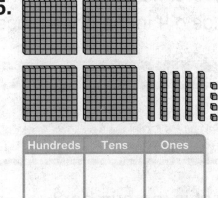

| Hundreds | Tens | Ones |
|----------|------|------|
|          |      |      |

_____

6.

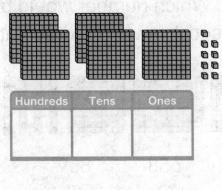

| Hundreds | Tens | Ones |
|----------|------|------|
|          |      |      |

_____

7.

| Hundreds | Tens | Ones |
|----------|------|------|
|          |      |      |

_____

8.

| Hundreds | Tens | Ones |
|----------|------|------|
|          |      |      |

_____

9. **Higher Order Thinking** Find the number. It has 4 hundreds. The digit in the tens place is between 2 and 4. The number of ones is 2 less than 6. _____

# Math Practices and Problem Solving
Solve each problem below.

10. © MP.7 **Look for Patterns** Complete the chart. A number has a 6 in the hundreds place. It has a 0 in the tens place. It has a 4 in the ones place.

| Hundreds | Tens | Ones |
|----------|------|------|
|          |      |      |

What is the number? _____

11. © MP.7 **Look for Patterns** Complete the chart. A number has a 4 in the hundreds place. It has a 7 in the tens place. It has a 0 in the ones place.

| Hundreds | Tens | Ones |
|----------|------|------|
|          |      |      |

What is the number? _____

12. **Higher Order Thinking** Choose a 3-digit number. Draw models to show the hundreds, tens, and ones for your number. Write the number below.

_____

13. © **Assessment** Max used these models to show a number. Which number would be shown if Max used 1 fewer hundred flat?

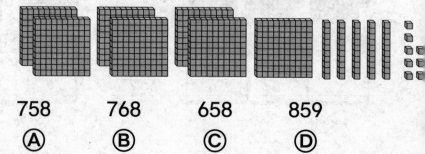

758        768        658        859
Ⓐ          Ⓑ          Ⓒ          Ⓓ

© Pearson Education, Inc. 1

Name _____

Solve

**Solve & Share**

Use the number line to skip count by 5s, starting at 0. Write the two missing numbers. Describe any patterns you see.

**I can ...**
skip count by 5, 10, and 100 using a number line.

© Content Standard 2.NBT.A.2
Mathematical Practices MP.2, MP.4, MP.7, MP.8

_____

_____

_____

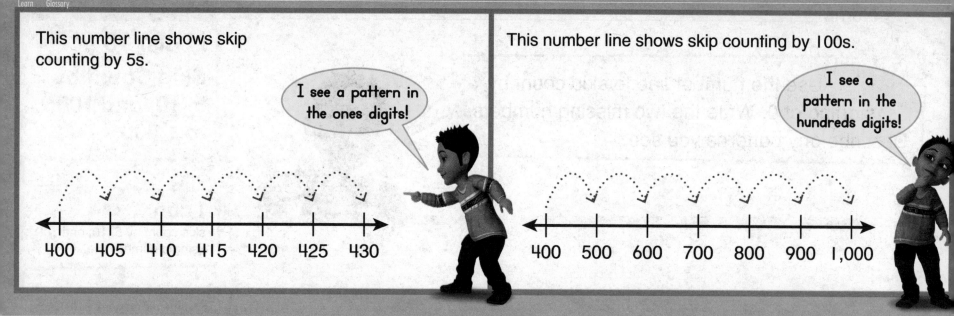

This number line shows skip counting by 5s.

I see a pattern in the ones digits!

400  405  410  415  420  425  430

This number line shows skip counting by 100s.

I see a pattern in the hundreds digits!

400  500  600  700  800  900  1,000

## Do You Understand?

**Show Me!** How could you use the number line in the first box above to skip count by 10s starting at 400?

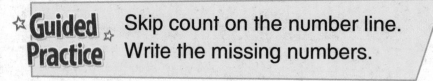

☆ **Guided Practice** ☆  Skip count on the number line. Write the missing numbers.

1.
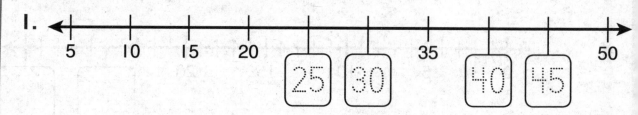

5   10   15   20   **25**  **30**   35   **40** **45**   50

2.
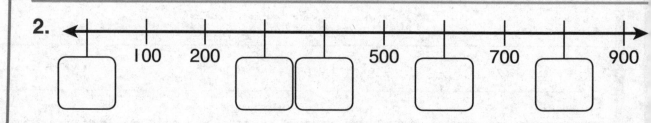

100   200            500        700        900

Name _____

**Independent Practice**   Skip count on the number line. Write the missing numbers.

3.

10 [ ] 30 40 [ ] 60 70 [ ] 90 100 [ ] 120 130

4.

400 405 410 [ ][ ] 425 [ ][ ]

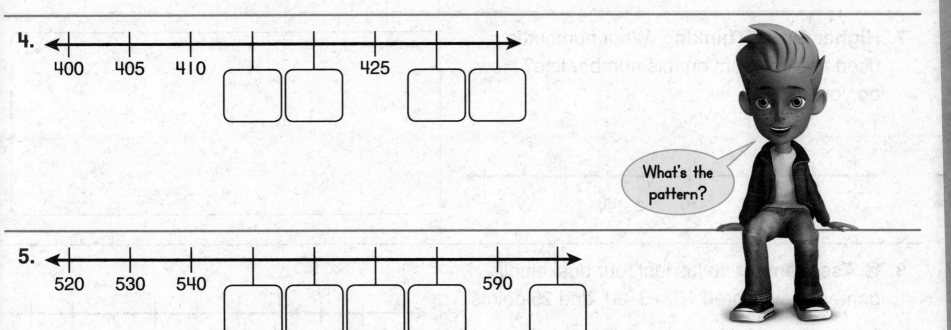

What's the pattern?

5.

520 530 540 [ ][ ][ ][ ] 590 [ ]

**Math Practices** and **Problem Solving**

Skip count on the number line. Write the missing numbers.

**6.** © **MP.7 Look for Patterns** Jill completed part of the number line. What numbers did she leave out? Complete Jill's number line.

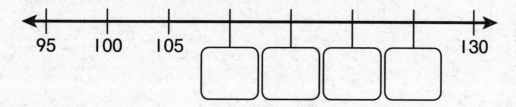

95    100    105    130

**7. Higher Order Thinking** What number is used to skip count on this number line? How do you know?

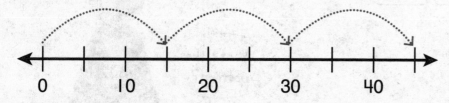

0    10    20    30    40

**8.** © **Assessment** In his last four basketball games, Roy scored 10, 15, 20, and 25 points.

By what number do Roy's points skip count?

5  10  15  20  25  30  35  40  45  50

   4          5          10         25
  Ⓐ         Ⓑ         Ⓒ        Ⓓ

# Glossary

**I less**

4 is I less than 5.

**I more**

5 is I more than 4.

**10 less**

20 is 10 less than 30.

**10 more**

10 more than a number has
I more ten or 10 more ones.

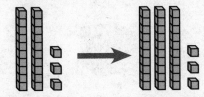

**add**

When you add, you find out
how many there are in all.

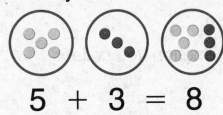

$$5 + 3 = 8$$

**addend**

the numbers you add together
to find the whole

$$2 + 3 = 5$$

**addition equation**

$$3 + 4 = 7$$

**addition fact**

$$9 + 8 = 17$$

## C

**column**

| 1 | 2 | 3 | 4 | 5 |
|---|---|---|---|---|
| 11 | 12 | 13 | 14 | 15 |
| 21 | 22 | 23 | 24 | 25 |
| 31 | 32 | 33 | 34 | 35 |

↑
column

**compare**

to find out how things are alike or different

**cone**

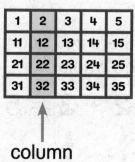

**corner**

**count on**

You can count on by 1s or 10s.

15, <u>16</u>, <u>17</u>, <u>18</u>
20, <u>30</u>, <u>40</u>, <u>50</u>

**cube**

**cylinder**

## D

**data**

information you collect

Favorite Pets
cat
dog
cat
cat
dog

**difference**

the amount that is left after you subtract

$4 - 1 = 3$

The difference is 3.

**digits**

Numbers have 1 or more digits.

43 has 2 digits.
The tens digit is 4.
The ones digit is 3.

43

**doubles fact**

an addition fact with the same addends

$4 + 4 = 8$
↑       ↑

4 and 4 is a double.

**G2**

## doubles-plus-1 fact

The addends are 1 apart.

$$\underbrace{3 + 4}_{\text{addends}} = 7$$

## doubles-plus-2 fact

The addends are 2 apart.

$$\underbrace{3 + 5}_{\text{addends}} = 8$$

**edges**

## equal shares

4 equal parts

## equal sign (=)

$$2 + 3 = 5$$

↑

equal sign

## equals

5 + 2 equals 7.

## equation

| | |
|---|---|
| 6 + 4 = 10 | 6 − 2 = 4 |
| 10 = 6 + 4 | 4 = 6 − 2 |

**faces**

## fact family

a group of related addition and subtraction facts

3 + 5 = 8
5 + 3 = 8
8 − 3 = 5
8 − 5 = 3

## fewer

A group that has less than another group

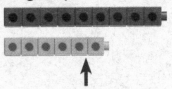

The yellow row has fewer.

## flat surface

## fourths

The square is divided into fourths.

## G

### greater than (>)

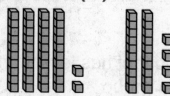

42 is greater than 24.

## greatest

the number or group with the largest value

| 7 | 11 | 23 |

23 is the greatest number.

## H

### half hour

A half hour is 30 minutes.

1:30

## halves

The circle is divided into halves.

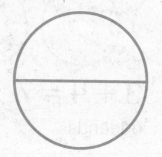

## hexagon

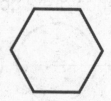

## hour

An hour is 60 minutes.

2:00

## hour hand

The short hand on a clock is the hour hand.
The hour hand tells the hour.

It is 3:00.                    hour hand

## hundred chart

A hundred chart shows all of the numbers from 1 to 100.

| 1 | 2 | 3 | 4 | 5 | 6 | 7 | 8 | 9 | 10 |
|---|---|---|---|---|---|---|---|---|---|
| 11 | 12 | 13 | 14 | 15 | 16 | 17 | 18 | 19 | 20 |
| 21 | 22 | 23 | 24 | 25 | 26 | 27 | 28 | 29 | 30 |
| 31 | 32 | 33 | 34 | 35 | 36 | 37 | 38 | 39 | 40 |
| 41 | 42 | 43 | 44 | 45 | 46 | 47 | 48 | 49 | 50 |
| 51 | 52 | 53 | 54 | 55 | 56 | 57 | 58 | 59 | 60 |
| 61 | 62 | 63 | 64 | 65 | 66 | 67 | 68 | 69 | 70 |
| 71 | 72 | 73 | 74 | 75 | 76 | 77 | 78 | 79 | 80 |
| 81 | 82 | 83 | 84 | 85 | 86 | 87 | 88 | 89 | 90 |
| 91 | 92 | 93 | 94 | 95 | 96 | 97 | 98 | 99 | 100 |

## I

## in all

There are 4 birds in all.

## inside

The dogs are inside the dog house.

## J

## join

to put together

3 and 3 is 6 in all.

## L

## least

the number or group with the smallest value

7   11   23

7 is the least number.

## length

the distance from one end of an object to the other end

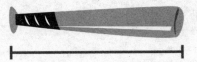

## less

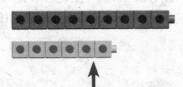

The yellow row has less.

## less than (<)

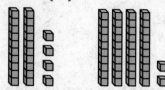

24 is less than 42.

## longer

An object that is 7 cubes long is longer than an object that is 2 cubes long.

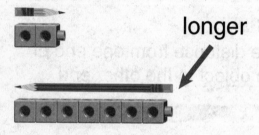

longer

## longest

The object that takes the most units to measure is the longest.

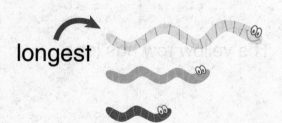

longest

## M

## make 10

7 + 4 = ?

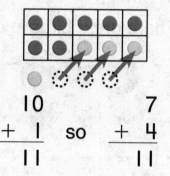

|  10 | | 7 |
| + 1 | so | + 4 |
| --- | --- | --- |
| 11 | | 11 |

## measure

You can measure the length of the shoe.

## minus

$$5 - 3$$

5 minus 3

This means 3 is taken away from 5.

## minus sign (−)

$$7 - 4 = 3$$

## minute

60 minutes is 1 hour.

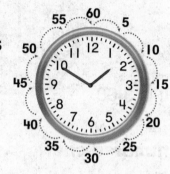

## minute hand

The long hand on a clock is the minute hand.
The minute hand tells the minutes.

minute hand

It is 3:00.

Glossary

## missing part

the part that is not known

2 is the missing part.

## more

The red row has more.

## near double

an addition fact that has an addend that is 1 or 2 more than the other addend

 $4 + 5 = 9$

$4 + 4 = 8$. 8 and 1 more is 9.

## number chart

A number chart can show numbers past 100.

| 81 | 82 | 83 | 84 | 85 | 86 | 87 | 88 | 89 | 90 |
| 91 | 92 | 93 | 94 | 95 | 96 | 97 | 98 | 99 | 100 |
| 101 | 102 | 103 | 104 | 105 | 106 | 107 | 108 | 109 | 110 |
| 111 | 112 | 113 | 114 | 115 | 116 | 117 | 118 | 119 | 120 |

## number line

A number line is a line that shows numbers in order from left to right.

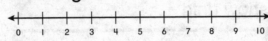

## o'clock

8:00
8 o'clock

## ones

The ones digit shows how many ones are in a number.

42 has 2 ones.

## ones digit

The ones digit in 43 is 3.

ones digit

## open number line

An open number line is a number line without marks in place.

## order

$$60 \quad 61 \quad 62 \quad 63$$

least            greatest

Numbers can be put in counting order from least to greatest or from greatest to least.

## outside

5 dogs are playing outside of the dog house.

## P

## part

a piece of a whole

2 and 3 are parts of 5.

## pattern

You can arrange 5 objects in any pattern, and there will still be 5 objects.

## picture graph

a graph that uses pictures to show data

| Favorite Pets | | | |
|---|---|---|---|
| Cat | Cat | Cat | Cat |
| Dog | Dog | Dog | |

## plus

$$5 \quad + \quad 4$$

5 plus 4

This means 4 is added to 5.

## plus sign (+)

$$6 + 2 = 8$$

## Q

## quarters

The square is divided into quarters, another word for fourths.

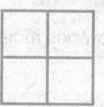

## R

## rectangle

## rectangular prism

### related facts

addition facts and subtraction facts that have the same numbers

$$2 + 3 = 5$$
$$5 - 2 = 3$$

These facts are related.

### row

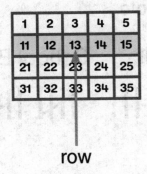

row

### scale

A scale is used to measure how much things weigh.

### shorter

An object that is 2 cubes long is shorter than one that is 7 cubes long.

 ← shorter

### shortest

The shortest object is the one that takes the fewest units to measure.

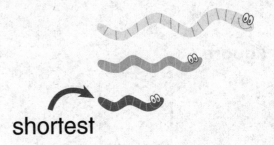

shortest

### side

These shapes have straight sides.

### sort

to group objects according to how they are similar

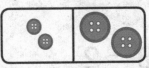

The buttons are sorted by size.

## sphere

## square

## standard form

a number shown in digits

28

## subtract

When you subtract, you find out how many are left.

$5 - 3 = 2$

## subtraction equation

$12 - 4 = 8$

## sum

$2 + 3 = 5$

↑
sum

## survey

to gather information

Do you like cats or dogs better?

Cats   |||
Dogs   ||

## take away

| Start With | Take Away | Have Left |
|---|---|---|
| 6 | 3 | 3 |

$6 - 3 = 3$

To take away is to remove or subtract.

## tally chart

a chart that uses marks to show data

| Walk | School Bus |
|---|---|
| ℍℍ || | ℍℍ ℍℍ |

## tally marks

marks that are used to record data

| Cats | 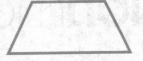 |
|------|-----|
| Dogs | II |

There are 5 cats and 2 dogs.

## tens digit

The tens digit shows how many groups of 10 are in a number.

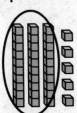 35 has 3 tens.

**35**

## Three-dimensional (3-D) shapes

These are all 3-D shapes.

## trapezoid

## triangle

## Two-dimensional (2-D) shapes

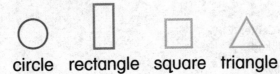

circle    rectangle    square    triangle

## V

## vertex (vertices)

a point where 3 or more edges meet

 vertex

## W

## whole

You add parts to find the whole.

5

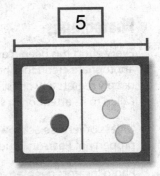

The whole is 5.

## Photographs

Every effort has been made to secure permission and provide appropriate credit for photographic material. The publisher deeply regrets any omission and pledges to correct errors called to its attention in subsequent editions.

Unless otherwise acknowledged, all photographs are the property of Pearson Education, Inc.

Photo locators denoted as follows: Top (T), Center (C), Bottom (B), Left (L), Right (R), Background (Bkgd)